The Hand Forged Knife

An Introduction to the Working of Modern Tool Steels

By Karl Schroen

Published by Knife World Publications
730 Broadway
Knoxville, Tennessee 37917

Photographs by Kerry Richardson

Layout and design by Kim T. Knott

ISBN 0-940362-08-2

Printed in the United States of America

Table of Contents

Preface

This treatise represents one blacksmiths's approach to knifemaking. Because this art form is so individual, the results using the same basic process are unique for each smith. Even with the rigid training of the Samurai sword smiths of Japan, the result of each smith was quite different. These differences can be accounted for by understanding the wide range of variables connected with the selection of materials (i.e., iron and steel), the forging of these, and finally the heat treating of the sword blade. In a similiar way, the use of modern steels presents a wide range of variables. To my knowledge, this is the first time ancient techniques of smithing have been combined with a full range of modern tool steels to hand forge knife blades.

This treatise is not limited to the forming of steel, rather the entire process of making a knife is explained in word, diagram, and photograph.

Traditionally, the blacksmith only shaped, hardened and tempered the knife blade. There were exceptions, but the rest of the finishing work i.e., polishing the steel and handle making, was usually done by others. For example, in Sheffield, England the hilt of the knife was frequently a silver alloy casting made by a jeweler.

In the modern world, access to new materials, information and machines has made it possible for one person to complete the entire process of making a knife. The modern cutler can thus use a variety of hilt materials to sculpt a wide range of shapes and sizes.

The art form is a very exacting one and demands a great deal of concentration. My objective is to combine the steel and hilt materials together into an object that looks like one piece with different textures. This inquiry contains enough information to be of use to both the beginner and advanced blacksmith.

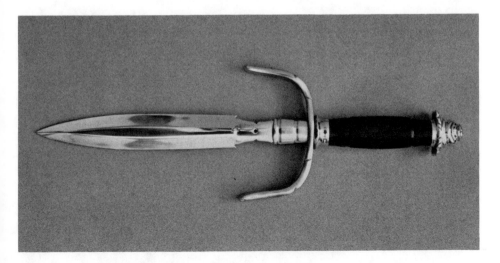

Background

I learned the fundamentals of blacksmithing from my father and was strongly motivated by stories told by him of my grandfather and great grandfathers, two of whom had learned their skills in Germany and emigrated to Michigan where iron and steel were in great abundance.

The first family shop that I saw was located in Saline, Michigan when in 1949 I visited there from California. The blacksmith shop was part of a larger building that also housed a hardware store. The shop was very large, having three forges and five anvils. From this shop, I am told that everything from plows to scissors were made and repaired. The hardware store served as an outlet for the products of the shop.

Here, as a youth, my father learned the elements of blacksmithing. He started by cleaning out the forges and building new fires. He later began to handle such tasks as filing and sawing hot and cold iron.

As the Industrial Revolution gradually replaced the need for hand work, Dad was encouraged to enter college. Quite naturally, he entered the field of mechanical engineering and received a degree from the University of Michigan in 1924.

Jumping a span of thirty years, in 1954, I entered college at the University of California at Davis. With Sputnik spinning around, I set out to get a job where I did not have to work with my hands. For some years, I tried to fit into the American Dream. I found, however, that the die had been cast long before and finally in the late 60's I stopped trying to fit into the whole scene. I decided to combine my early training in blacksmithing with a background in science. The result had lead me straight into the field that is the subject for this study.

I have often thought that all those years spent were merely a preparation for my present endeavor. In any case, I do not think that I would have been drawn into this type of enjoyable life without the two threads of my past coming together.

Dedicated to my father, C.K. Schroen

Introduction

Nowadays, if you ask most people what a blacksmith is, they invariably say horse shoer. If you ask people what a cutler is, you get a blank look. In the space of less than one hundred years, an entire group of people has become obscured to the point of almost non existence.

Say we were walking down the street of Anytown USA in the year of 1879. One of the most prominent buildings in town would be the blacksmith shop. If the smith was trained formally i.e., in an apprentice program, he might be skilled in both of the specialty forms of the blacksmith's art. One day he may work as a farrier, shoeing horses, and the next, making knives as a cutler all day.

If Anytown was of a large size, the blacksmith might list himself in the town register as a cutler. His products might include table knives, butcher knives, swords, sickles, scythes, lancets, buttons and buckles, corkscrews, tailors' shears, dentist equipment, and many other tools.

If Anytown, on the other hand, was small in size, the smith might have to perform any and all tasks of the trade. Such was the condition of one of my great grandfathers. John Hauser was a German trained blacksmith who specialized in making watch parts. When he moved to Saline, Michigan in 1870, he found that it was impossible to carry on with his former trade. He soon became a general blacksmith in that small town.

The shop itself was one large room with a dirt floor and only one window. In the middle stood a brick forge with a long leather bellows attached to it. My father said he watched for hours as the bellows pumped air through the chunks of hot coal to heat the iron or steel in preparation to hitting it with a hammer. The large anvil stood on a stump next to the forge acting as the forming table to receive the blows of the hammer as it shaped the hot metal. Aside from the anvil, which was cast in a foundry, all of the other tools in the shop were made by John Hauser. These included a wide assortment of tongs, hammers, and many other tools of the trade.

The iron used in the shop came from the iron ore dug from the mines in the upper part of Michigan. I have a hammer made by John Hauser from iron and steel that was smelted in his shop. Because steel was so hard to make with their limited equipment, they used it sparingly.

Looking closely at the hammer we see the back is made of wrought iron. Wrought iron is made by infusing relatively pure iron with iron silicate. It is easy to work and contains a small amount of carbon. So small an amount that it will not harden. For that reason, John hammer- welded a piece of steel onto the face of the hammer. Unlike the wrought iron with its siliceous slag fibers, steel contains more carbon and no slag. It is easy to work and will harden. To do that, after he was through welding the two metals together, John reheated the steel surface and dipped it into a bucket of water.

In the corner of the shop was a large cast iron stove. Cast iron is iron with lots of carbon in it (2.4 percent). The main difference then in the composition of wrought iron, steel and cast iron is the amount of carbon each contains-

1

wrought iron has the least and cast iron has the most.

Steel is an alloy of iron and carbon. An alloy is a substance made of two or more metals and/or one or more nonmetallic elements. Carbon and silicon are examples of non metal alloying elements.

The iron to make the steel no longer comes from the once iron rich upper Michigan mines. Now, low grade ore is re-processed to make steel. The carbon comes from coal that has been partly burned and made into coke.

The shop that I now have is quite different than that of my great grandfather's of 80 years ago. I specialize in knifemaking. I do, however, still use a coal forge, hammers, anvil, and tongs. This equipment will be described later; but first I will describe the materials that I use.

Tool Steel

The steel that I use for making knives is a far cry from that which my great grandfather used in the early part of this century. In fact, even today, only a small fraction of the steel produced is the ultra high processed tool steel. By far the most steel produced is structural steel used in the building of autos, fences and buildings. Structural steel comes in a wide variety of compositions and sizes. Most of this steel is low in carbon content, has dissolved gases in it and in other ways, is not desirable for making knives.

For the utmost in purity, strength, and reliability, tool steel today is produced in a type of electric furnace to which a vacuum is connected.

What is Steel?

If we were to take a piece of steel from the scrap pile behind my great grandfather's shop and in some way take it apart, we would find that it was mostly made of iron. The steel to which he had access was rather simple. The only intentional addition to the iron was carbon. The carbon is not just floating around in the iron but is actually hooked to the iron in a substance called a compound. The name of this compound is cementite. (Fe_3C)(figure a)

Another way of looking at it is to compare the weights of each element in the compound. It is easy to feel the difference in weight between a piece of charcoal (which is almost pure carbon) and an identical piece of iron. The iron is much heavier. In fact, the iron weighs almost five times as much as the carbon. We know that carbon weighs 12 and iron weighs 56, when compared to hydrogen which weighs 1. In cementite, for each 12 pounds of carbon, you have to add 168 pounds of iron ($3 \times 56 = 168$). In other words, a little carbon goes a long way. Too little carbon and you have wrought iron, too much and you have cast iron.

One way to see this relationship of carbon to iron is to fill a gallon glass jar with water. Now add one drop of ink. Soon the ink will work its way to all parts of the jar. It takes a very small amount of ink to discolor the water just as it takes a small amount of carbon to change the iron to steel. Carbon is by far the most important alloy in steel.

All modern steels have, in addition to carbon, other elements added to the iron. Even what is called a straight carbon steel has the elements silicon and manganese added. A straight carbon steel may be low in carbon (.10 percent), medium (.30 percent) or high in carbon (.60 percent) and more. Knives are made of high carbon steel of very high quality. This is the type of steel that I will discuss in this study.

Tool steel as used here is high quality, high carbon steel that is used to make tools. It is a crystalline solid that, when heated to a certain temperature, changes form; the solid crystals of iron change to form a solid solution. The room temperature iron, called ferrite, starts to come together with the iron carbide, called cementite, at 1335F to form the solid solution called austenite. At this temperature, the cementite abruptly begins to dissolve in the iron.

3

In other words when you stick a piece of steel in the forge and let it turn red then orange and start to hit it, you are hitting steel in its austenite phase. If you continue to heat the steel to a yellow color and beyond to the white incandescent colors, the iron in the steel changes to crystalline form again as you watch it melt. Taking the steel out of the fire and letting it cool down once again, the steel changes back to ferrite and cementite.

Steel then is a form of iron to which a small quantity of carbon is added. All modern tool steels contain, in addition to carbon, other alloy elements which alter the steel in specific ways: 1. produce greater strength in large sections, 2. provide less distortion in the hardening process, 3. add greater abrasion resistance to the steel, 4. provide higher toughness and at the same hardness levels when the pieces are small, 5. retain strength at high temperatures.

Understanding the fundamental metallurgy of iron and steel is, I believe, essential for the bladesmith interested in working with modern tool steel. The brief explanation that I have written is intended to introduce the subject in a practical way. I will continue to relate techniques which have been built upon a thorough exploration of theories and facts gathered over the years.

Forging

Forging of the steel is very important because it not only shapes the material but refines the grain structure. When enough steel crystals are combined to become visible, they appear as small sandlike particles. The size of these grains is dependent on temperature, steel composition, and mechanical (hammering) forces. The grains increase in size with heat; thus during most of the early hammering, the size of the grains is large. As the steel is forged, the size of the bar is changed and, in the case of a knife blade, becomes thinner. As this happens, it requires less heat and lighter hammering to effect a change in the bar shape. The grains meanwhile are aligning themselves into parallel rows in the direction that they are being forged. (figure b)

The final refinement of the grain size is referred to as grain refinement and is done by the smith at the same time that the final shape of the bar is finished. Grain refining the steel is very important and involves hammering the steel at a dull red color for a long period of time. Grain refinement in parallel rows is essential for strong, high quality cutting edges. The smaller the grain size, the stronger the material. (figure c)

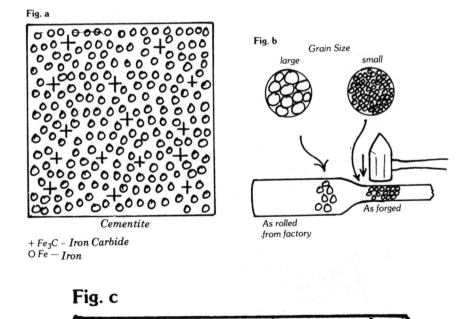

Fig. a

Cementite

+ Fe$_3$C - Iron Carbide
O Fe — Iron

Fig. b

Grain Size

large   small

As rolled
.from factory

As forged

Fig. c

grain refinement

Annealing

The forging of the tool steel in order to produce a fine grain size, has at the same time created great stress in the bar. The various methods used to relieve stress are collectively known as annealing. There are many types of annealing. I will discuss one of those kinds called spheroidize annealing that best describes what is taking place inside the bar of tool steel. It may be added, that as the stress is relieved in the steel, the bar becomes softer and more easily shaped with a file, grinder or drill.

The mechanism for spheroidize annealing involves the bladesmith's application of just the right amount of heat at the proper time. The spheres are small particles of carbide that have not yet dissolved in the iron to form austenite. These undissolved carbide spheres form the center on which the smith hopes to add more carbides so that the bar will be filled with these spheroidite structures interspersed in a background of soft pearlite. Pearlite is the soft crystalline structure of the steel at a temperature range of 1000F to 1335F just before it changes to austenite. 100 percent pearlite does not machine or harden well, so the smith uses undissolved carbides in the pearlite to open it up and become a more desirable material.

Each time the bar is reheated to the dull red to red range (1000F to 1335F) and then cooled slowly, more spheroidite is formed. Thus, combining the grain refining operation, which disperses the carbides, with the dull to red heating produces a very sound piece of tool steel. I continue the heating and cooling cycle for some time after the packing has been completed, then bury the bar in a pre-warmed trough of sand and spent coke. The bar is thus ready to be ground to shape, sanded, drilled or tapped and finally hardened. (figure d)

Fig. d

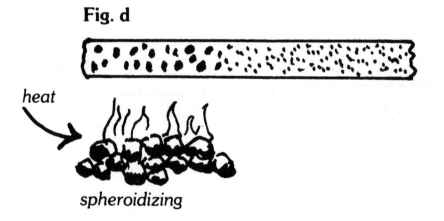

heat

spheroidizing

Hardening

The hardening of high carbon tool steel is the process by which austenite is converted to a needlelike crystalline form called martensite. Martensite is the desired end product of the hardening process. It forms directly from austenite. The amount of martensite formed is directly related to the amount of carbon that the steel contains. The more carbon- the more martensite.

In plain carbon tool steel, martensite starts to form from rapidly cooled austenite at about 400F. The temperature of the austenite at the time of cooling is 1500F. The steel is quickly cooled in order to avoid soft or otherwise undesirable structures in the steel that form at temperatures between 400F and 1500F. The first undesirable structure to form below 1500F is pearlite. At 1335F pearlite appears, under the microscope, as wavy lines that are arranged in parallel rows. This structure lasts until about 1000F at which time it starts to change to a feathery structure called bainite. Bainite changes gradually as the temperature is lowered and near 400F has needlelike spines similar to martensite. This lower temperature bainite is the only desirable crystalline structure besides martensite that should be present in the hardened steel. Bainite is desirable because it lends toughness to the hard martensite.

There are two ways of avoiding the temperature ranges that produce undesirable crystalline forms. The first and most simple is to lower the temperature of the steel from 1500F to 400F so quickly that pearlite and other undesirable products do not have time to form. This method is the traditional water quench. Other quench liquids employed to drastically lower the temperature are brine (salt water) and various types of oils. The cooling rates vary from fastest in brine to slowest in oil. (note: I use Imperial "S" quenching oil, which is distributed by O.L. King, Div. of Far Best Corp.) This oil cools fast enough to harden the steel but avoids the sudden changes of water or brine which can cause the steel to crack.

A second method for transforming austenite to martensite is used in modern tool steels. This relies on the addition of alloys such as chromium and molybdenum, to name two, that stabilize the austenite and thus carry it to lower temperatures. If austenite can be held, without converting to pearlite, then the rapid, drastic quench can be eliminated. This is exactly what happens in those steels with proper amounts of the alloys added. The austenite is carried to a lower temperature and finally, in less than one millionth of a second, shears off to form martensite. The term commonly applied to this process is "Hardenability". Certain steels, to be discussed later, are alloyed in such a way that they will harden in still air after being raised to their hardening temperature, i.e. Air Hardening Steel.

The term hardenability also implies another interesting relationship that happens in the hardening process. Simple high carbon tool steels with only small amounts of silicon and manganese in them will not harden all the way through in a water quench if their diameter is larger than about 1-1/2". But, for example, if a small amount of molybdenum is added, the steel will harden all the way through.

I have successfully hardened many kinds of water, oil, and air hardening steels in an open forge fire. Details will follow later.

Tempering

As with the forging operation, the hardening of the steel leaves the steel in a very stressed condition. For this reason, steps are taken to relieve that tension and, at the same time, retain a maximum amount of hardness. If the knife blade is not tempered immediately after hardening, the hard brittle steel will shatter like glass if subjected to a sudden shock or blow.

Tempering is the reheating of the hardened steel to a temperature below the hardening temperature that partly softens the steel. Along with this softening, the internal stresses are relieved.

The tempering process has been complicated somewhat through the use of modern highly alloyed steels. These steels have so many complex carbide systems in them that they actually create new, smaller grains when heated beyond the normal tempering range of water hardening steel, i.e. 300- 400F. These new carbides form very actively from 800 to 1000F and increase the initial hardness of the steel a great deal. Since they are new, they too require stress relief. So with these steels, it is always wise to double temper after hardening.

The tempering techniques that a bladesmith acquires rely mainly on his ability to develop to a high degree of intuitive sensitivity to the steel and constant practice.

There are no incandescent colors to go by because the steel does not get hot enough to show them at the tempering temperature. The oxide colors, those colors that are caused when the shiny steel on heating is changed, are only partly reliable. I say partly because there is a time lag between the appearance of the oxide and the actual temperature of the steel. This time lag gets longer as the temperature is increased.

I have trained myself to use a series of sharp and dull files to judge the hardness that I desire.

This chart illustrates the four basic processes necessary to make a knife from high carbon tool steel: forging is necessary to shape the steel; annealing to relieve the stress created by forging; hardening and tempering respectively make the steel hard and then tough.

Forged steel is of two parts: Over half of the steel is iron or ferrite; carbon is present as iron carbide or cementite. On heating, steel forms austenite at 1333F. This is the non-magnetic steel the smith hammers on.

Slowly cooled after forging, the steel changes to a soft crystalline form, pearlite (1000F). Bainite forms at about 800F. The steel returns to ferrite and cementite at room temperature.

Annealing softens the steel. The diagram shows the softest form of steel is formed at temperatures above and below the critical temperature due to the large carbides called spherodite embedded in a background of pearlite. This soft, open structure is retained at room temperature. Also the hardening of high carbon tool steel involves the change from austenite to marten-

High Carbon Steel Chart

Temp	Forging		Annealing	Hardening	Tempering
	Slow Heating	Slow Cooling	Annealing	Hardening	Tempering
1600°F	Pure Austenite (orange)	Pure Austenite		Pure Austenite	
1435°F	↑ (red)	↓	Austenite		
1335°F	dull red		+ Carbide		
(dull red)	very dull red	Pearlite	Pearlite +	↓	High Temp Zone
1000°F	↑	↓	Sperodite	Rapid Cooling	
800°F		Bainite			
550°F		↓	Martensite +	Low Temp Zone	
400°F	Ferrite +	Ferrite +		Retained Austenite	
200°F	Cementite	Cementite	↓		
70°F				Sub-Zero Quench	
-70°F					

site, which is the type of crystal that makes steel hard. In steels of lower alloy content, i.e. W-1, O-1, hardening requires the drastic lowering of steel temperature in order to avoid the temperatures where pearlite is formed. Steels with higher alloy content skip the pearlite zone by slowing the cooling rate on the way to forming martensite. This time lengthening by alloys is known as hardenability. High carbon, high alloy steels sometimes require sub zero quenching because they retain a large amount of austenite at room temperature (up to 30 percent). This room temperature austenite is very unstable, changing to marteniste so quickly that the steel will warp and crack. The only way to avoid this non uniform change is to eliminate it as soon as possible after the steel reaches room temperature. I use acetone and dry ice to lower the temperature to -70F. Some tool and stainless steels seem to respond well to very low sub-zero treatment i.e., -300F. The whole field of cryogenics has altered our view of conventional heat treatment. (See technical manuals in the back for references on this subject.) Once the steel is hard, it is also brittle. Brittleness is taken away from the steel by tempering. Lower alloy high carbon steels require tempering temperatures up to 450F to soften. Steels of higher alloy content have larger quantities of brittle carbides that require higher tempering temperatures, i.e., 1000F.

The Blacksmith Shop

The appearance of the blacksmith shop has changed through the years as new equipment such as modern welding machines have taken its place. The basic tools, however, have not been replaced. The forge, anvil, hammers and tongs are still essential tools no matter what the smith is working on. The space has also changed very little. There is still the requirement for subdued

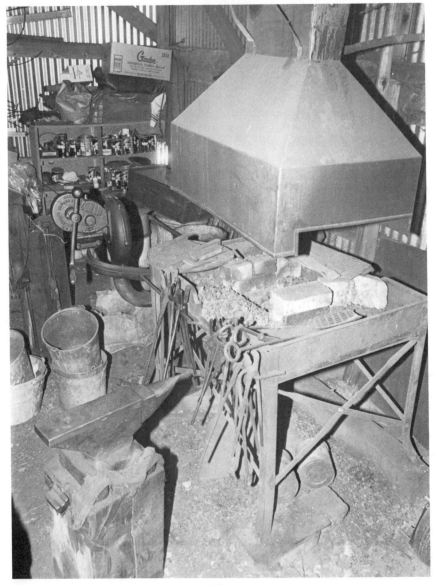

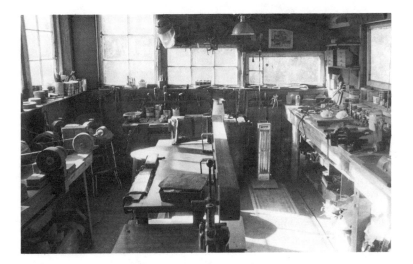

light and a non flammable floor. From this point on, the modifications begin to reflect what specific work the smith is centered on and perhaps just as importantly, the personality of the blacksmith.

I have been in blacksmith shops that were so clean you could, as they say "eat off the floor". On the other hand, I have seen shops that defied description, where it would be necessary to dig a path from the forge to the anvil. My shop is someplace in between these two extremes. Since I have a great liking for the out of doors, my shop or forging operations generally take place outside by a shaded wall or under a tree. I use a forge made by the former Champion Blower and Forge Co. of Lancaster, Pennsylvania. Obtaining these sturdy centrifugal masterpieces remains a mystery to me. Generally, when I stop looking, someone will contact me out of the blue and I will receive another gem. Once received, the restoration begins.

Breathing New Life into a Forge Blower

Briefly, to acquaint you with a hand operated forge (see diagram), there is a cut away illustration of the simple mechanics of the blower with its relationship to the rest of the forge. The main point of this is to furnish the fire with a constant supply of air. Since the smith turns the operating crank by hand, it stands to reason that the most efficient gear mechanisms are the best. I have omitted the use of electrically run forges because I cannot get the control needed to avoid over heating the tool steel.

There are made a wide variety of forges which I will not attempt to describe. However, some general tips, I feel, are in order. First, when examining a blower, turn the crank. If you have difficulty, or if you hear a grinding sound, stop. Most probably the bearings are stuck with heavy grease that is so old that it is on its way to stone. I have found that the easiest way to loosen this grease is to remove the cover plate over the gears and lower the entire blower into a tub of solvent. I use kerosene. In most cases, the grease will loosen easily. The bearings have covers that either unscrew or have sleeve fittings. Remove the covers and take out all the old grease. This is time consuming and if you want to remove the roller bearings, you can loosen the retaining nut and slide the whole assembly out. When all the bearings have been replaced, run solvent through the entire moving mechanism. This flushing action generally removes any remaining grime.

Next, remove all the explosive solvent and put new grease in the ball bearings. You now have a new machine. Incidently, if any of the ball bearings are out of round or badly scored, they can be replaced with a visit to an auto parts store.

Some bearings may be gummed up so badly that solvent will not work. Then, with all solvent removed, use a propane torch to gently and evenly heat the bearing cap. When the cap is removed, let it cool and continue with the solvent treatment.

Blacksmith Forge Cut-Away

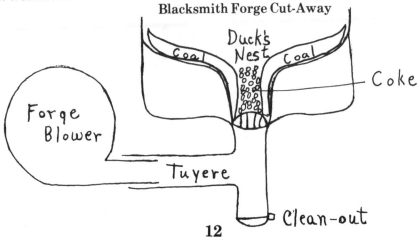

Forge Body

The forge body is connected to the blower by way of a hollow tube called the tuyere. Just before it enters the forge itself, this tube diverges; one way leads to the forge, the other to a clean out trap. The air is forced up the tube, through the grating and into a pocket called the duck's nest. This nest area varies in size depending upon the the type of forge you have. These basket shaped places contain and concentrate the forge fire. The heat generated in them is so intense that they must be built of heavy cast iron or fire brick. My thin walled portable forge will soon need a new floor because the one that it came with was made of a thin gage metal.

I have found an excellent way to both preserve new forge bodies and repair old ones. A high temperature bonding mortar called Hiloset, made by Kaiser industries, works well to insulate and protect the forge pot from burning out. Of course, the old standby of 1 part mortar to 9 parts fire clay also works.

The Anvil

The anvil is a massive piece of steel or iron that serves as a work table for blacksmiths. Up till the turn of this century, anvils were very common in this country. They came in all different sizes and shapes. Now they occasionally appear out of the dusty corners of old barns and workshops.

Most of the anvils that I have seen within the last few years are made of hardenable carbon cast steel. The quality of the new cast anvils from Sweden that I have seen is poor. The faces are almost uniformly soft and require much valuable time to work harden, i.e., grain refining the surface with light blows to eventually harden it. The other option is to harden or have hardened the surface of the anvil to a depth of at least 1/2 inch.

Some anvils, including the one I use, have a welded, hard steel plate on the surface. Mine is an excellent anvil and has stood up since I got it 10 years ago. The quality of the welding job is the key for the success of this type of anvil.

The most important single part of the anvil is the face. I have worked on a wide variety of different anvils, but what is essential to me is a smooth flat surface. Since most operations that I do with an anvil involve the face, I do not need or often use the horn (note: high carbon tool steels do not lend themselves to bending operations).

There are two holes in the face of the anvil, one round and one square. The round hole is called the pritchel hole and is used by horseshoers to fashion inserts for horseshoes. The square hole, or hardy hole, is used by a wide number of anvil tools. This square hole locks and holds the tool in place.

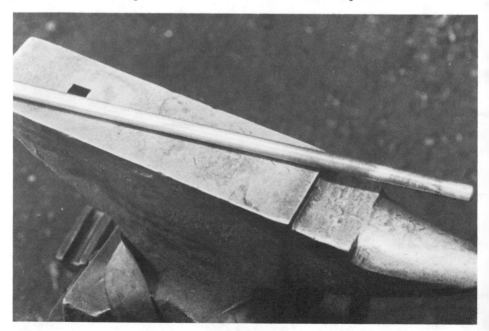

The surface of the anvil is hardened steel and is therefore subject to cracking and chipping if improperly used. My father told me to treat it like glass since it is so difficult to repair. So far, I have never chipped or damaged an anvil. Most old anvils that I have seen obviously were never used by people my father would have gotten along with. It is difficult to ruin an anvil, but I have seen more ruined ones than good.

Two rules that I learned very early were: firstly, for every 100 pounds of anvil, use no more than a 10 pound hammer. Secondly, always strike hot steel on the anvil with the hammer face parallel to the anvil face. The hammer head and anvil are both hardened steel and will chip or crack if improperly connected. In fact, they should never come in contact with each other when in use.

Hammers

The blacksmith's hammers are his main tools for shaping the steel. They are simple of shape, but very complex and subtle in the hands of an experienced smith. The shapes and sizes are directly related to the intended use.

The most common hammer universally used by blacksmiths is called the cross peen hammer. The handle is situated midway between the head and the

slant sided peen. This hammer is used to lengthen, bend, and flatten steel. Moved in one direction, the peen is employed to widen a piece of steel.

Every specialized part of the blacksmith's art has its own hammer styles. The cutler is no exception. Like any experienced blacksmith, the cutler does not rely upon one hammer, but uses a whole series of hammers. The real secret to hammer use is when and how to use the right one. I have found that modern tool steels have forced me to abandon the traditional, general shape, forming hammers like the cross peen for heavier double faced hammers.

The reasons for the change to these hammers comes from the various stages required in the forming of a knife blade. The steel starts generally as a round rod. The round rod will be squared, elongated, and flattened. Remembering that the steel is extra tough, I start the forging with the largest, double faced hammer that I can find to match my 100 pound anvil. I therefore start my hammering with a 10 pounder.

With the crude shape finished, I move to the specialized cutler's hammers. Many smiths have never seen this type of hammer. Regardless of weight, these hammers have a universal shape. Most of the weight is distributed on one side of the handle. The face is extremely awkward if you do not know how to use it. This is a superb hammer for shaping, flattening, and packing tool steel. Holding the handle about 6 inches from the head, the hammer fairly walks back and forth along the steel. The trick is to get the hammer to do the work with as little actual lifting of the arm as possible. I use two such hammers, one 6-1/2 pounds with a narrow head and a 7 pounder with a wide head.

When the steel has been forged thinner and flatter, I use a 3 pound, double faced hammer for the corrective shaping. The shape and smoothness of the blade. is determined by the smoothness of the contacting surfaces of the hammer and anvil. The temperature of the steel is also very important. The details of hammering as well as all the specific techniques of forging will be given later.

Tongs

Tongs are an extension of the hand to be used to hold a piece of steel that has become too hot to hold with the hands. I revert to the tongs when I have to. Tongs are more awkward to use than the steel rod. The variety of tongs is endless. A glance into any old fashioned blacksmith's shop is staggering. The smith makes a tool to make a tool. My father said that, in the course of a large project, several pairs of tongs would often be made and used.

There is nothing different about the tongs I use today. The selection from the wide variety of shapes is, however, very specific. Tongs that hold tool steel must fit so tightly that little if any turning motion of the steel is possible. Tool steel is difficult to hold, especially while you are hitting it. It is imperative to have the proper tongs to lock the steel in place.

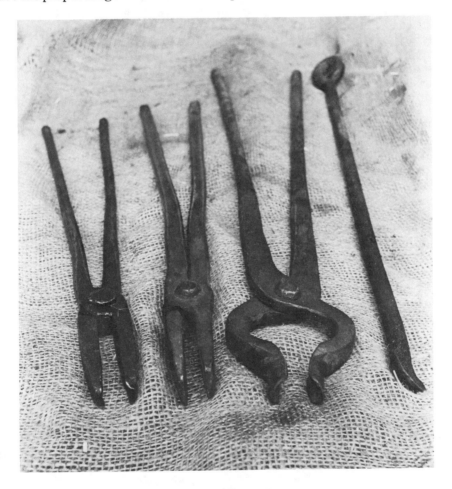

Coal

Coal is a traditional fuel used by blacksmiths to heat their iron and steel. Coal is present under the earth's crust practically wherever plants existed; therefore, virtually every major area of the world contains coal. Coal is compressed, decayed vegetable matter. Since there was a wide variety of plants on the earth millions of years ago, with a wide range of chemical makeup, so, too, there are a great many different types of coal.

Coal is divided into major groups which are based upon the length of time and the conditions under which the coal was deposited. Anthracite, or hard coal, has been in the ground the longest and contains the most carbon. Bituminous, or soft, coal has less carbon. A third form, lignite, contains the least carbon. Bituminous coal has undergone the decay process for less time than anathracite and, therefore, contains less carbon than anthracite.

The conditions under which the plants were deposited is very important in determining the chemical make up of the coal. Pressure and temperature have created, over the years, an assortment of products in the coal. These products determine the burning qualities of the coal, i.e., volatility and amount of BTU (British Thermal Unit). One BTU equals the amount of heat required to raise 1 lb. of water 1 degree F. There are also a number of inorganic components of coal which are of particular importance to the blacksmith. Sulfur content of coals is of particular interest to the blacksmith. Sulfur, when burned, combines with oxygen to produce caustic oxides which are harmful to the steel (and smith). The blacksmith, therefore, looks carefully at the analysis of the coal to see that the sulfur content is 1.0 percent or less.

Ash content is another inorganic characteristic of coal. It is made of many minerals that, when heated in the forge, make what is called a "clinker." These clinkers form mostly on or over the grate. They slow down the free flow of air into the fire. I have found that an ash content of 10 percent or more is very undesirable. Here, as in sulfur content, the lower, the better. Clean coal means clean tool steel. The lower the sulfur and ash content, the better.

The most desirable coal that I have found is called metallurgical coal. It consists of special bituminous coal or mixtures of bituminous and anthracite. A typical analysis of this coal is: Carbon 55 to 75 percent, Moisture 2 to 5 percent, Ash 2 to 12 percent, Sulfur .5 to 3 percent, BTU 13,000 to 16,000 and Volatile matter 25 to 30 percent.

When buying smithing coal from the local feed store, it is wise to ask if they have an analysis of the coal and to look at the coal. If the coal is in chunks and has yellow lines running through it, that is probably sulfur. If the coal is in powdered form, does that mean that it is high grade metallurgical coal or just the dust swept off the floor of a coal mine? The best thing to do is try a small amount before you buy it. Good coal will form lots of slow burning coke and put out plenty of heat. Chunk coal requires no special preparation unless the pieces are, say, over an inch in diameter. I then hammer it down. I like chunk coal mainly because I do not have to use much water with it.

Fire Building

Unlike chunk coal, powdered coal requires water to shape and form it. The idea is to make a paste of the coal and build it into ridges surrounding the grate so as to create a hollow cavity into which is put kindling.

As the fire progesses, the sides that you have constructed start to burn and create a furnace. If I want an oven effect, I put the paste coal over the fire. The fire so constructed with good coal will last a full working day with minor adjustments. I also like to build the sides parallel to each other so that the knife blade can be shoved through the fire without contacting the moist coal because wet coal can crack tool steel in the forge. Water, in excess, in the fire area is harmful to the surface of the steel. I mention this because blacksmiths working with mild steel and wrought iron tend to use a lot of water to control their fire. This practice with tool steel can be disastrous.

As the fire begins to heat up, the coal is carbonized to coke. Coal that is capable of producing this light expanded product in large volumes is much sought after by smiths because it represents that much more potential heat energy. Some smiths acquire coke from places where it is made, i.e., steel mills, and burn it directly in their forge. Since it is unlikely that you will use all the coke that you produce in one day, the excess coke can be saved and used to start and maintain subsequent fires. Once you have the proper coal, the proper construction and maintenance of the forge fire is essential.

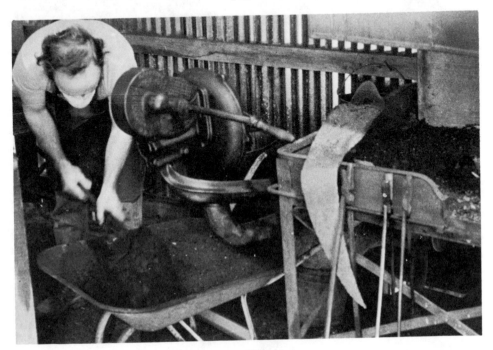

Tool Steel

This section is intended to furnish to the blacksmith information that is largely unavailable to him elsewhere. I have drawn technical information from tool steel manufacturers and research work that is strictly geared to industrial application.

The challenge is and has been to use simple, direct methods to effectively forge, anneal, harden, and temper these materials, using the tools commonly found in a blacksmith shop.

Eight or nine years ago I started to experiment with high carbon alloy tool steels. At first I did so in a random fashion with no particular reason for selecting a steel other than I had heard or read about it. Since I was used to the blacksmith's standby or water hardening steel, I soon found that these other steels did strange things. After about two years of intensive, and at times frustrating, work I began to learn how to adjust my techniques. I found that I did not have to change any of the familiar smithing tools so much as I had to alter my attitude toward the new material that I was using. The benefits are most rewarding because since then I have successfully worked with every main category of high carbon tool steel currently in production.

I have selected 15 of these steels as being representative of the 7 general categories of tool steel. In one case I used 5 steels from the same category.

Classification
of Tool Steels

Entire books on the classification and designation of tool steels are available. I will present basic information to give the smith a working knowledge of the subject.

Tool steels are classified in three ways: by chemical composition, by mechanical properties and by usage. The two organizations responsible for these codes are the Society of American Iron and Steel Institue (AISI) and Society of Automotive Engineers (SAE).

The SAE system consists of a long number and letter code based on the chemical composition of the steel. I find the lists hard to use because it is difficult to associate so many numbers with a specific steel and its usage or mechanical properties.

The AISI has, in the past, presented the various tool steels in categories that include all three types of classification. What follows is an explanation of their six major divisions and a separate category altogether, i.e., stainless steels; note that each division has a letter symbol that helps to identify that group:

    1. W...Water hardening tool steel
    2. S....Shock resisting tool steel
    3.   Special purpose tool steel
       L...Low alloy type
       F...Finishing type (carbon- tungsten)
       P...Plastic mold type

4. Cold work tool steel
    O...Oil hardening
    A...Air hardening (medium alloy type)
    D...High carbon high chromium type (die steel)
5. Hot work tool steel:
    H1 thru H19...Chromium based types
    H20 thru H39...Tungsten based types
    H40 thru H59...Molybdenum based types
6. High speed tool steel:
    T...Tungsten based types
    M...Molybdenum based types

This kind of grouping combines chemical composition, method of hardening, and usage altogether. The system evolves into a more elaborate network of numbered classes. The classes are a method of expanding the main divisions and allow for new steels to be included. For example, the traditional water hardening steel is in class 110 with an AISI designation of W-1. The class numbers go from 110 to 660. If the steel is or has been produced, it is given an AISI number or designation to match its class number. The steels that I will evaluate in this article have type and class designations as follows:

AISI Type	Class Number
W-1	110
L-6	232
S-5	313
S-1	320
O-1	410
A-2	420
D-2	430
M-2	650
154CM, 440C, 440V	
Bg42	
ATS-34, CPM-10V or A11	
Vasco Wear	

The hot working steels, plastic mold steels and the finishing steels were not included in my evaluation. The first two are not used to make knives and the last is no longer available. In addition to the steels listed above, I have also used and evaluated a seventh general category, namely, stainless steel.

Briefly, there are three kinds of stainless steel produced in the United States today: Austenitic, Ferritic, and Martensitic.

The first two steels, as their names indicate, will not form martensite and thus will not harden. Martensitic stainless is a high carbon tool steel with a large amount of chromium added to prevent rust and corrosion.

I have selected martensitic stainless steels as being representative of the group, i.e., 440C, 154CM, Bg42, 440V, and ATS-34. They contain more than 14 percent chromium. I have found that lesser amounts of chromium make the steel stain resistant, not stainless. (Note: Stainless steels have their own separate classification system. Since I have only used one type, I will not explain this coding.)

25

Steel Evaluation

The first high alloy tool steel that I began to experiment with was D-2. As it turned out, it was also the hardest to master. Hammering W-1 was like hitting a soft sponge in comparison to D-2 which felt like a stiff pine board. All the other steels tested arranged themselves somewhere in between these two extremes. A close runner up to D-2 is 154CM which feels about the same.

My next move was away from the forge and into the University library. It seemed to me that the key to understanding the new steels was to understand the alloy systems which made them behave the way that they did. What I found out involved much more than just understanding each of the eight alloys in the steel. I had opened a can of worms, so to speak, that I found most interesting and rewarding. I now realize that with the understanding comes the ability to truly get the most out of the material. Certainly, a large part of this art form has to do with manipulating in very subtle ways a material that is extremely difficult to shape using traditional blacksmithing techniques.

I now realize that what made the Samurai sword smiths great was not necessarily the mechanics of their process, but rather, that they understood and directly related to the entire process. By selecting the proper raw materials to begin with, they as much determined the final outcome of the smithing as anything that was to follow.

I will start the steel evaluation with the alloying elements as this is the most obvious place. Note: Not every element is present in each steel. Elements used as alloys and their symbols are: Carbon-C, Manganese- Mn, Silicon-Si, Chromium- Cr, Molybdenum- Mo, Tungsten- W (wolframit), Vanadium- V and Nickel- Ni.

W-1 Water hardening steel- C 1.05, Mn.25, Si.25
S-5 Shock resisting steel- C .60, Mn.85, Si 1.90, Cr.25, V.2, Mo.30
S-1 Shock resisting steel- C.55, Mn.25, Si.25, Cr 1.25, V.20, W 2.75
L-6 Low Alloy Steel- C.75, Mn.70, Si.25, Cr.80, Ni 1.50, Mo.30
O-1 Oil hardening steel- C.90, Mn 1.35, Si.35, Cr.50, W.50
A-2 Air hardening steel- C 1.00, Mn 1.00, Si.30, Cr 5.25, V.30, Mo.80
D-2 High carbon High chromium die steel- C 1.55, Mn.25, Si.38, Cr 12.00, V.80, Mo.80
Vasco Wear- C 1.12, Si 1.20, Mn.30, W 1.10, Cr 7.75, Mo 1.60, V 2.40
M-2 High speed- C.85, Mn.30, Si.30, Cr 4.15, V 1.95, Mo 5.00, W 6.40
154CM Martensitic stainless steel- C 1.05, Mn.50, Si.30, Cr 14.00, Mo 4.00
440C Martensitic stainless steel- C 1.00, Mn 1.00, Si 1.00, Cr 17.00, Mo.75
Bg42- Martensitic stainless steel- C 1.15, Si.30, Mn.50, Cr 14.5, Mo4.00 V 1.2
CPM-IOV- C 2.45 Si.90, Mn.50, Cr 5,25, V 9.75, Mo 1.30
440V- C 2.2, Si.50, Mn.50, Cr 17.5, V 5.75, Mo.50
ATS-34 - C 1.02, Si.15, Mn.41, Cr 13.66, Mo 3.50

General Evaluation

It turns out that the forging qualities are not the only things affected by changes in the amount and variety of alloying elements. All the other operations, i.e., annealing, hardening and tempering, are in some way affected.

By using each of the 15 steels in the four operations listed above, and then comparing them to their alloy contents, I could predict how each would function. These 15 steels of known values may furthermore be used as standards for unknown steels.

The most difficult part was relating the incandescent colors to temperatures. I used a simple pyrometer to obtain actual temperatures:

Degrees	Color
800	Dull black-gray
1000	Dull red (first color) still grays
1100	Dull red, no other color
1200	Dull red, brighter
1300	Dull red, still brighter
1400	Red
1500	Deep red
1600	Orange red
1700	Orange yellow
1800	Bright orange yellow
1900	Yellow orange
2000	Light yellow

The colors were observed in the typical subdued light near the forge area in most shops. These judgements are subjective since it is hard to define subdued light. Note: Pyrometers are available in ceramic shops where one can also learn how to calibrate pyrometers.

Much of my early work was done by trial and error without a pyrometer. The experience was extremely valuable because I found ways to accurately judge temperature by incandescent color that were later confirmed when I used the pyrometer. I also established the fact that forging, annealing, hardening and tempering of the steels listed can be done on an open fire. The only permanent damage that could not be changed came when the steel was overheated or struck at the wrong temperature regardless of the heat.

Alloy Analysis

CARBON has by far the greatest influence of any of the alloys. Steel could not exist without carbon. Martensite, along with bainite give steel a microstructure of hard, tough carbide. None of the other elements so dramatically alter the strength and hardness as do the small changes in carbon. Carbon iron crystalline structures have the widest number and variety known to exist in metallurgy. They also combine with other elements to furnish steel with an assortment of iron alloy carbide systems.

MANGANESE is in all produced steels. Here, it is used as an agent to remove oxygen from the steel. Oxygen forms harmful oxides in steel. This alloy also keeps the steel from being ruined while working it hot. Manganese is used in moderate amounts in tool steel to increase hardenablility (0.2 to 0.4 percent). Higher amounts used to increase hardenability have the disadvantage of having more austenite retained at room temperature after hardening. Austenite formed this way is very unstable and can change abruptly in the steel, thereby creating cracks.

I have observed that in L-6, O-1, A-2, and 440C where the carbon and manganese are high, tempering times are long and at times unpredictable. These steels, with the exception of L-6, also have a tendency to crack when forged in small sections. They may also crack when they are being twisted or hot cut. Cracking occurs in the red zone.

SILICON, like manganese, is used as a deoxidizer in tool steel. If the amount of silicon is high, i.e., 1.0 percent or more, and the carbon content is moderate, i.e., .40 to .60 percent, the tool steel will be very tough, e.g., silicon shock steel. But on the other hand if both silicon and carbon are high, i.e., 1.0 percent, then free carbon (graphite) may form. Graphite may cause cracking while forging tool steel. Silicon differs from manganese in that it raises the critical temperature and thus the hardening temperature. Silicon does not lower the start of martensite formation.

Tool steels like S-1 and S-5 are extremely tough but have a tendency to scale when forged, even at lower temperatures. However, they harden and temper easily with no sudden change in hardness. With the exceptions of 440C , S-1, and S-5, the other steels that were tested have moderate amounts of silicon. 440C contains a high percentage of silicon (1.0 percent) for strength, hardenability, and corrosion resistance.

CHROMIUM is an important alloying element present in all but one of the steels that I used (i.e., W-1). In small amounts (.25-.50 percent) chromium increases hardenability and reduces soft spots common in water hardening steels. In moderate amounts (.80 to 1.25 percent) it retards corrosion and oxidation. In percentages of 4.0 percent and more abrasion resistance is added to the above qualities. Stain resistance is supplied by 11 to 12 percent chromium. Chromium above 12 percent is necessary for stainless properties in high carbon tool steels. High chromium content does not seem to necessitate excessively hard forging. D-2 with 12 percent chromium is much harder to forge than 440C with 17 percent chromium.

NICKEL is present in only one of the steels used. However, it seems to have outstanding characteristics for imparting toughness at relatively high carbon content. L-6 was one of the finest steels that I worked into a knife blade. In lowering the hardening and tempering temperatures, nickel minimizes the chance for quench cracking and distortion of long thin blades. Nickel also lowers the degree of rust which eventually causes the steel to pit.

MOLYBDENUM is mainly used to give greater hardenability to the steel. Even low amounts (.20 to .30 percent) greatly increase the depth of hardening in steel (e.g., L-6 and S-5) and at the same time, retard what is called temper brittleness. The alloy also prevents high temperature stress (creep) both while forging and high temperature tempering.

TUNGSTEN has properties similar to those of molybdenum. Perhaps the outstanding function of tungsten is wear reistance. Tungsten carbides carry this wear-resistance to red hot temperatures (e.g. S-1 and M-2).

VANADIUM was added to steels originally to scavenge slag impurities in the processing of steel. It was found that the alloy greatly increases the wear resistance of steel. Vanadium carbide is one of the hardest structures in tool steel. Vanadium carbides have very fine grains but dissolve in the austenite only at high temperatures. Therefore, to take full advantage of them, the steel must be heated accordingly. Fortunately, the fine grains of vanadium carbide prevent grain coarsing at high temperatures. Note: Grain coarsing at high temperatures is a prime cause for failure in the tool making process, i.e., during the forging and heat treating.

Evaluation of the 12 Tool Steels used in This Study

Note: All forging was done with the same 3 lb hammer and the anvil and tongs were prewarmed to prevent stress cracking; a very important point.

W-1 Water hardening tool steel is the basic tool steel traditionally used by bladesmiths. It behaves much like low carbon mild steel. W-1 is the easiest steel to work and can be bent, twisted, and forged into more kinds of shapes than any of the other steels tested. It is however, easily burned by overheating. Many blacksmiths that have been trained to work their steel hot cannot adjust to lowering the forging heat to a red orange instead of a bright orange to yellow. Not only does the steel scale and pit when worked too hot, but the grain structure is coarsened which eventually weakens it.

As with all tool steel forging, do not use much water to control the burning of the coal as it will not only cause the steel to scale, but to crack as well if accidently pushed into a wet spot. I use a wire brush and washing borax to control the formation of the scale.

W-1 is simple to harden and temper and is the only steel with the exception of O-1 that can be tempered using the traditional oxide colors to judge the hardness. I prefer to use the file for determining hardness.

I have found that for knife blades, heat treating oil gives far more consistant results than the water quench. If regular quenching oil is not available, use a clean, light motor oil, e.g., 10 wt. Light oil is not only easier to move the steel through, but it has a greater cooling action than the traditionally used crank case oil.

Since W-1 is a shallow hardening steel, larger pieces, e.g., hammer heads, should be quenched in water or brine.

I have made many knife blades from this material and can say that aside from the fact that it rusts, W-1 blades hold an excellent edge and above all are very simple to sharpen.

S-5 The outstanding thing about this steel is its toughness at a high hardness level. S-5 is also versatile in that large sections may be water quenched, e.g., hammer heads. The high silicon content (1.90 percent) slows the softening process during tempering of this steel. The steel forges much like W-1. But, there is a degree of stiffness under the hammer which makes S-5 slightly more difficult to forge. The 0.30 percent molybdenum makes the steel somewhat air hardening. This means that every time the steel is removed from the fire, it starts to harden; that is why it appears to be stiff under the hammer and to lose heat faster than other steels. In order to prevent cracking, slow the force of the hammer blows as the steel loses heat. If the steel starts to crack near the edges, you know that your technique is at fault. The only exception comes when you are grain refining the steel in the final stages of blade shaping.

I have had good luck with this steel. It is similar to W-1, but tougher in small sections.

O-1 is a universally used oil hardening tool steel. The most outstanding quality, to me, is the edge holding properties of O-1. It forges like S-5; in fact it is hard to distinguish the two steels. Manganese is the dominant alloy in this steel. This alloy lowers the start of martensite formation so that there may be some unchanged austenite in the steel after it is hardened. I have found that the trick with O-1 is to cool it quickly in cold oil to eliminate as much austenite as possible and to temper immediately.

O-1 has the habit of requiring a long time to temper and will change its hardness level unpredictably and suddenly. This means that you have to be alert and constantly check the hardness levels with the files.

Other than the obvious cares taken when hardening O-1, this steel is an excellent choice for knife blades. It is easily available from steel suppliers in a range of sizes and shapes. A-2 discussed later, has very similar tempering properties to O-1. (A-2 has a 1.0 percent manganese content.)

S-1 is not a steel used to make knives because it contains a low .5 percent carbon. This amount of carbon gives an insufficient amount of martensite to the blade. The steel is very important because it can be forged into hot punches and other hot working tools. I use S-1 for making sharpening steels for carving sets. It is a very tough tool steel, so tough in fact, that I frequently skip the tempering step by quenching it in warm oil (approx. 50C- 120F) briefly and removing the steel before it has reached the oil bath temperature, and letting it air cool.

The dominant alloying element in S-1 is tungsten. Tungsten not only gives this steel its hot working qualities, but makes it noticeably more difficult to forge than the three steels previously discussed. The amount of this alloy varies from 2.0 to 3.0 percent, depending on the steel maker. Since tungsten has some of the same qualities as molybdenum, S-1 will crack if hit too hard near the edge of thin sections.

L-6 is my favorite steel. It is relatively easy to forge and scales very little if kept in a clean fire. The knives that I have made from L-6 are very tough and easy to sharpen. The carbon content is sufficiently high (.75 percent) to insure good waring qualities. The combination of nickel, chromium, and molybdenum form a superb balance of alloys that insure high strength, toughness, and hardenability. The low hardening and tempering temperatures give a greater margin of safety than for the other tool steels used in my evaluation. L-6 forges much like S-1 and it is debatable which one is stiffer under the 3 pound hammer.

There are two different types of L-6 on the market. The main difference between them is that the one I have used for the evaluation contains molybdenum and the other does not. Carpenter steel L-6 contains no molybdenum. This steel forges slightly easier than the Crucible steel's L-6 which has molybdenum. The molybdenum variety requires more care in forging to prevent cracking and because of the higher hardenability, in the latter steel, tempering times are longer. My personal perference is for the Crucible variety because the edges hold their sharpness for a longer time.

A-2 is a popular, tough, air hardening tool steel. Air hardening means that no drastic quench, i.e., oil or water, is necessary in order to harden the steel. Instead of quenching this steel, it will harden by removing it from the fire at an orange yellow color and letting it cool in still air. I have found that this steel will become harder if you harden the steel twice. In other words, bring the steel to the same color to harden twice with a cooling to room temperature in between the two heatings. Then I temper the blade twice to remove retained austenite.

Another way of hardening A-2 is to super cool it in a bath of acetone and dry ice (-70 degrees F). This step is done after the hardening and cooling process. Temper twice after this is done. Note: Never dump dry ice in acetone but slowly pour acetone over the dry ice.

I have used A-2 for several years and like its non warping properties especially when making thin razor like blades.

Vasco Wear is a new tough, wear resistant cold work die steel. This steel forges easily, i.e., like S-5. Scaling during forging is moderate. Annealing, grinding to shape was easy with this steel. Hardening was likewise easy. (Note: Although this steel is air hardening, I found that an oil quench worked to harden the steel better and also increased its toughness). The real problem with this steel showed up in the finishing room. Vasco Wear polishes and sands with great difficulty. When polished, it is not stainless and the edge is extremely hard to establish. Vasco Wear is an appealing tool steel because of its tough, wear resistance and good edge holding ability, however, it is too expensive to finish and polish.

M-2 is a high speed steel that has outstanding properties of edge holding. High speed steels have very high alloy contents compared to the other tool steels. These additions give M-2 excellent wear resistance. Chromium, tungsten, vanadium and molybdenum are the alloys which give M-2 these characteristics. For all of this, the steel forges reasonably well. The usual care must be given to prevent cracking at low temperature forging.

The amazing thing about M-2 is that, at the hardening temperature, the color is in the yellow orange range (2000F). This temperature range would cause burning in the steels so far discussed. Solution of the carbide forming alloys in the steel is essential to get the most out of their additions. It is, however, easy to overheat these steels in the forge. Slow, even heating to temperature is the only way that I have found to avoid overheating and excessive scaling.

Tempering of these steels requires careful attention to heating rates just as in the hardening process. The tempering of this steel can be done at two general temperatures (400F and 1000F). I have had good results with tempering at 400F twice. The steel, unlike the more simple W-1 and O-1, becomes harder after the second tempering as more and more retained austenite is changed to martensite.

At elevated temperatures, i.e., 1000F, maximum hardness is attained. I am not convinced, however, that the steel is any tougher as a result of this high temperature tempering. I have found that it improves the toughness of this steel to quench the steel after it has been tempered at these temperatures in order to avoid a condition known as temper brittleness which is encountered at 500F-700F. I use a preheated slab of steel to bring the blade up to the proper temperature.

M-2 is not a steel for the beginner bladesmith. It requires close concentration at all levels of working. The steel is also very expensive ($8.00 a pound). But make no mistake, this steel has some outstanding qualities. Among these are wear resistance, toughness, and edge holding ability, the best I have seen in any steel currently used for making knife blades.

D-2 is a familiar cold work die steel to knifemakers having been around for many years. Originally, I forged D-2 from flat stock. I found, however, that a fair amount of grain separation occurred using flat stock. I then switched to round stock and the problem was eliminated. I believe that there must be a difference between flat and round stock that comes from the factory, (grain structure).

As with other high chromium steels, i.e., stainless, I preheat all tools that come into contact with the steel during the forging, (hammer, tongs, and anvil). The secret to forging these steels is to keep the forging temperature as low as possible.

D-2 is an excellent knife steel. The steel is reasonably inexpensive ($5.00 pound), finishes with relative ease and has very good edge holding qualities.

440C is a popular, stainless steel for making knife blades. It is used extensively for this purpose by industrial cutlery firms. The blades that I have made from 440C have given much better performance than those factory made knives that I have tested. By that I mean that my blades were easier to sharpen and held up longer than the others tested.

The classic, universal complaint that I have heard about stainless steel is that knives made of it do not hold an edge well and do not sharpen easily. I would certainly agree with these complaints in general. But I have found that the fault does not seem to be caused by the material but rather by the techniques or process used in making the knives. The issue is further complicated because there are a number of different types of martensitic stainless steels manufactured and it would be hard to sort out all of the many variables connected with the problem. Add to all these things the fact that many stainless steel knives come from foreign countries and the problem becomes impossible to unravel.

Forging 440C is difficult because it has a marked tendency to crack. The high silicon and manganese (both 1.0 percent) may account for this response. The addition of 16 to 20 percent chromium to a 1.0 percent carbon steel, I believe, may also account for the fracturing.

Once I solved this problem with lighter hammering at a reduced temperature, the cracking problem was solved and I began to get good, consistant results. The steel is still difficult to forge. One common mistake that is made by the beginner is to try to hammer on this material vertically after it has been flattened. The trick is to do as much of the blade shaping and drawing while the steel is narrower in circumference. This rule holds for all of the tool steels that have high hardenability ratings. This is one reason that I leave the tip of the blade flattened. The other reason is that it allows a greater radius to the point. (See Diagram D -Knife Finishing Procedures)

The hardness of this steel drops off too much for my liking after 400 degrees F so I do not temper 440C at elevated temperatures. I have found that the toughness of this steel is improved with a double temper at 400 F.

154CM is martensitic stainless that has come out of the space associated industry. In addition to cutlery, the steel is also used to make ball bearings. I have found that it makes an excellent stainless knife steel. It has similar finishing properties to 440C but does not crack under the hammer as much. This is not to say that it is not hard to forge. This steel moves very reluctantly. I would say that it is the hardest steel physically to forge of those tested. The same precautions must be used with it as in the other high alloy steels.

I have found tht 154CM responds nicely to heat treatment; I use successfully both the double hardening techniques developed for the air hardening steels and the sub zero quench method to eliminate the retained austenite.

Bg42 is a Latrobe Steel product that is similar to the Crucible Steel 154CM.

Bg42 contains vanadium and 154CM does not. Both steels are stainless. The working qualities are very similar in both steels. The edge holding ability of Bg42 is slightly better than 154CM but the price of Bg42 at $15 to $16 a pound is very high. The steel is a pleasure to work and finish.

ATS-34 is the Japanese version of 154CM. After working the steel for some time, it seems to forge more easily than 154 CM and ultimately produces a tougher, longer lasting edge than 154 CM. It has excellent edge holding properties and would make a good steel for kitchen knives.

440V. This steel, while sharing a similar designation to 440C, has a very different type of chemical makeup. With more than double the carbon content and a large amount of vanadium, this steel is more like D-2 than 440C when it come to wear resistance and toughness. The steel also has the advantage of being stainless. 440V forges hard but evenly, much like D-2.

CPM-10V has a very high carbon and vanadium content which gives it exceptional wear resistance. The edge holding ability of this steel is amazing, however, the steel will rust quite easily. Finishing and polishing the steel is difficult and time consuming. The advantages to me far outweigh the disadvantages.

The above sketches of the steels that I have used should give the bladesmith some idea of the material that is used to make knives. Every steel has its good and bad points. There is no perfect material. I have found that if the steel responds relatively well to start with then the results will be good. The rest depends on the skill of the smith and just getting used to the particular steel. Modern tool steels are valuable materials for the traditional bladesmith who wants to take the time to understand them.

Forging Operations: Forging

The term forging has to do with the shaping of a bar of steel while it is hot. I will show how I forge a round bar of tool steel into a shape that resembles a knife blade. After this crude shape has been silhouetted on a grinder and sander, I will demonstrate how the blade is hardened and tempered.

The diameter of the tool steel that I start with depends on the width and thickness of the knife blade that I want to make. (Note: each round lengthens from 1" to 3" from its original dimension). As a rule of thumb, 1/2" round stock flattens to 1" wide by 1/8" thick and 3/4" flattens to 1-1/8" wide by 3/16" thick. (Note: be sure to smooth the ends of the rod before forging to prevent cracking).

I generally make a rough sketch of the knife shape before I start. Next, I cut off a piece of round stock about 1-1/2 feet long. I arrange the forge, anvil, hammers and tongs in close proximity to each other for the quick easy movements necessary when working with tool steel. Most tool steels, when cooled, become rigid and hard to move with the hammer.

The proper heat is essential in all four steps of the forging operation. My approach is to work the steel at the lowest possible temperature for any one step, i.e., forging temperatures are kept close to 1800F in a range from 1800F to 2000F. This range of forging temperatures holds for all 12 tool steels that I use. The color is bright orange. As the steel is reduced and changed in size, the temperature is lowered accordingly (i.e., 1800 degrees down to 1000F finishing). The object of this careful attention to heat is to preserve a small grain size– the smaller the better. If the steel is forged at too high a temperature, all of the subsequent steps, i.e., annealing, hardening, and tempering will be adversely effected.

The forge fire that I have built has now gotten up to temperature and I now slip blocks of steel into the fire in order to heat the anvil surface. I next place a grate over the fire to heat the hammers. When the anvil surface is warm, the hot blocks are used to warm the sand and spent coke (small particles of spent coke help to remove water from the sand). The sand is on the annealing plate.

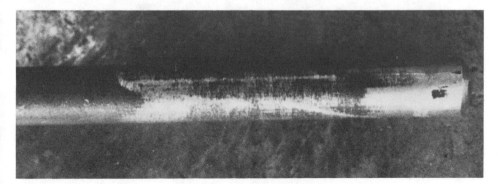

Preheating of the anvil and hammers greatly reduces the chance for cracking in the forged tool steel.

The forge fire is now ready to receive the tool steel rod. As the steel comes to an orange color, I remove it and with even flat blows, begin to square the end—not too hard at first— so that when the steel stops moving, I stop hammering. Each side is parallel with its opposite. Laying the big 10 pound starting hammer on the anvil, the steel is gently returned into the fire. Without disturbing the fire, I remove the annealing plate and set it aside and return to the flow of watching the steel constantly and squaring the end that will soon be about 3" long and ready to fit my small hollow bit tongs. I also occasionally wire brush the scale off the steel before returning it to the fire.

I reach for my cut off hardy and slip it into place. With ruler and file, I remove the steel and hot file the spot to be cut off on the hardy, returning the steel to the fire and positioning it over the fire, where the cut is to be made. As the steel heats, placing the small tongs on the anvil ready to hold the cut off piece of steel, and looking for that yellow orange cutoff color, I remove the steel, squaring it over the hardy, hitting it one, two, three, four times until the steel is almost cut through. Then, lifting off the hardy and putting down the hammer, I use the tongs to twist off the steel and stick the round rod into the sand and the half made knife blade into the fire. I next wait for the steel to come up to forging temperature again.

The squared end sticking out of the fire will become the tang or support system for the hilt (handle). When the heat is up in the steel, it is removed with the tongs, and the hand cranked fire dies down, aiding the low forge temperature. In two heats, the sides are trued and the tip is widened. (See Diagram A.) The blade is kept uniform in dimension and slowly flattened. Now the larger hollow bit round tongs are used to grab the steel.

First, the blade end is flattened, then the tang, as the steel grows longer and flatter. (See diagram B.) The 10 pound hammer gives way to the cutler's hammers- the 6-1/2 pounder for subtle shaping, the 7 lb. hammer for flattening the sides. The tang needs continual squaring with the 3 pounder, and the rhythm is constant until the blade is smooth and flat (45 minutes to 2 hours). All the while that the blade is becoming thinner, the heat is cut down until, at the final flattening, the color is a dull red (1000F).

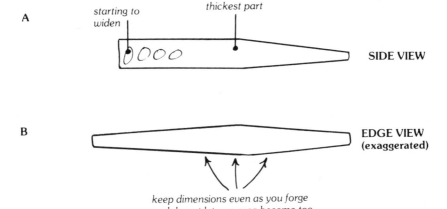

A

starting to widen

thickest part

SIDE VIEW

B

EDGE VIEW
(exaggerated)

keep dimensions even as you forge and do not let one area become too thin in relation to the other

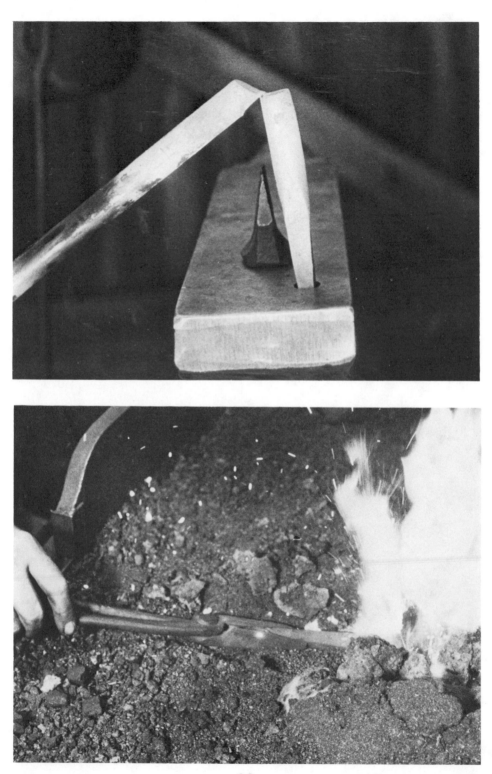

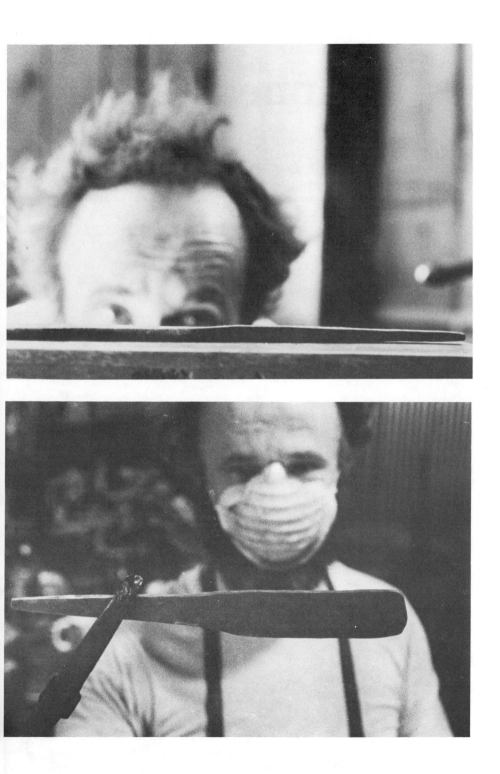

Annealing

At last, the blade is flat enough and the annealing pan is again over the fire. The blade is heated to a dull red if it is of low alloy steel, or to red, if of high alloy. After 6 or 7 passes in the fire, the blade is finally shoved vertically into the sand and the annealing has begun.

In 15 or 20 minutes, I remove the blade and check for hardness with a dull file. See diagram C. I also look for cracks or chips due to faulty forging techniques, e.g., edge cracking or pitting from too hot a blade hit too hard perhaps with the wrong hammer. If the blade is uniformly soft, i.e., easy to file with the dull file, I then grind and smooth the blade.

C

check with dull file for softness

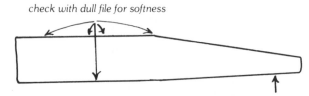

Note: if threading tip of tang, be sure to soften if needed

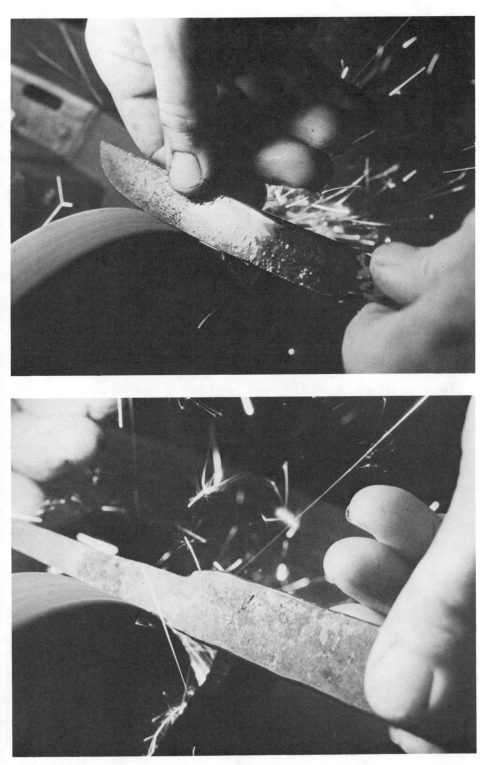

Hardening and Tempering

After the blade is ground and sanded to shape, it is ready to be hardened and tempered. The purpose of hardening is to increase the strength of the tool steel. But once hardened, the steel is too brittle to use, so it is necessary to slightly soften it in such a way that its strength is still maintained.

The process has been done traditionally by the bladesmith in the forge. I go to a lot of trouble to see to it that the fire and the steel are properly prepared.

The fire should be long enough to accommodate the blade and at least one half of the tang. My common rivet forge is adapted for this purpose by the use of two steel bars and a long grate resting on top of them. With chunk type coke, I build a long, high mound using no water to bind the coal when the fire is started. Water oxidizes the steel and should always be avoided in the heat treating fire when possible.

Since it is impossible to build a fire using powder coal without water, I mix, build and burn this type fire for some time to eliminate as much water as possible. For the oven effect I can either put a plate over the fire or use coal mounded over it.

The blade is next coated with borax to protect it from oxidation in the fire. Borax (i.e. the washing type) was traditionally used both as a flux in welding and as a coating material to protect steel from the oxidizing effects of the fire. I take a coffee can and fill it with 1/3 borax and 2/3 water. I put it on the fire over the grate or on a separate fire, and as it rolls to a boil, I dip the blade into the supersaturated solution. Once dried, the blade is ready to harden. Now, read the following flow sheet carefully:

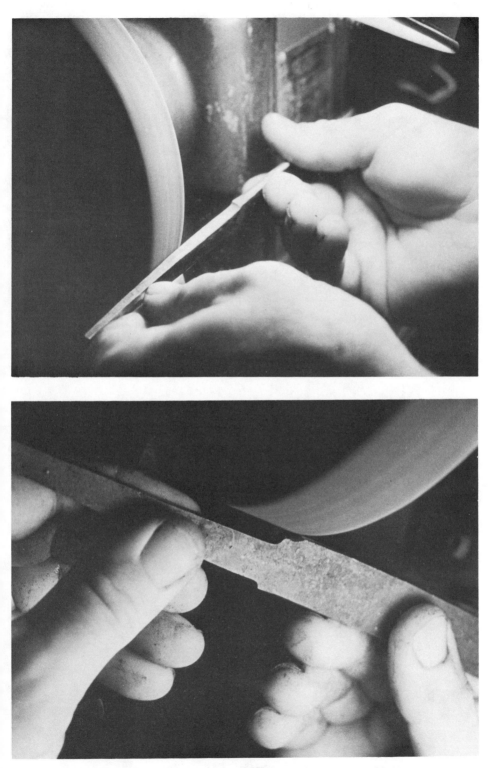

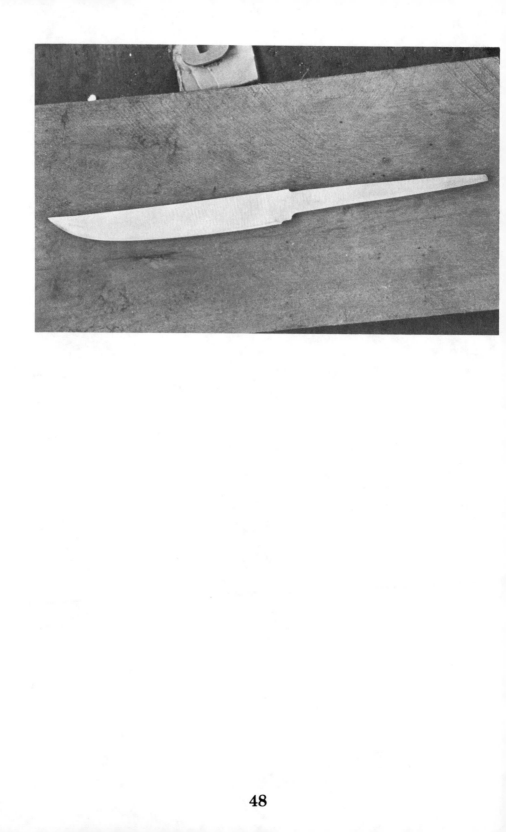

Steel vs Incandescent Colors- Flow Chart

Group I- W-1, O-1, S-1, S-5, L-6: harden slowly from dull red to red; let soak for several minutes without turning crank on blower. Quench in Imperial S quenching oil (5 gallons) prewarmed to not more than 120F (W-1 to 130F). Temper immediately. These steels change quickly. (Imperial S is a medium range quenching oil.)

Group II- A-2, D-2: put in fire that is orange to yellow orange; let soak, remove and air cool. Then bring it to a dull red and cool. In other words, double harden with stress relief in between. Double temper to 400F (Note: alternative procedure is to sub zero quench in acetone dry ice, after first hardening, to reduce retained austenite; skip second hardening. (See diagram D).

Group III- 154CM, 440C, M-2, Bg42, Vasco Wear: Preheat steel to red and remove; heat fire to yellow orange for 5-6 minutes and let steel soak until evenly heated. Remove and quench in room temperature Imperial S quenching oil. Temper 400F to 1000F. 154CM especially benefits from sub zero quenching. Sub zero quench is not necessary for 440C as it has a tendency to crack. For M-2, use a longer soaking time or double harden at an orange yellow. Quench in cold oil if necessary to harden. (i.e., room temperature)

D

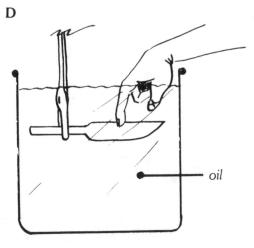

finger on blade to see
if cool — do not remove
if too hot to touch

49

Hardening Technique

The hardening process, once the fire is built, is essentially the same for all the tool steels that I have used. The big differnce between the three groups is the intensity and duration of the heat. As the steels become more complex, i.e., higher alloy amount and variety, the temperature is raised to disperse and dissolve the alloying elements. This is especially true of the so called refractory alloys such as chromium, tungsten, molybdenum and vanadium, which retain their strength at high temperatures.

Secrets of Successful Forge Hardening

1. Get the heat in the forge that is desired for the particular steel without the blade being in the fire.

2. Do not overheat. Remember that the steel can be heat treated again if not hot enough, but is ruined if overheated. Note: if steel does not harden the first time, bring to a full, dull red, put in sand tray to anneal, and harden over again.

3. Move steel constantly in the forge oven to make sure the blade and at least one half of the tang is evenly heated.

4. Move the blade gently and evenly in the quench until it is the same temperature as the oil. Note: put a finger on the blade while in the oil. (See Diagram E.)

5. Use dull, then sharp file around the edges of the knife to check hardness, especially in the area near the junction of the tang and blade. (See diagram F.)

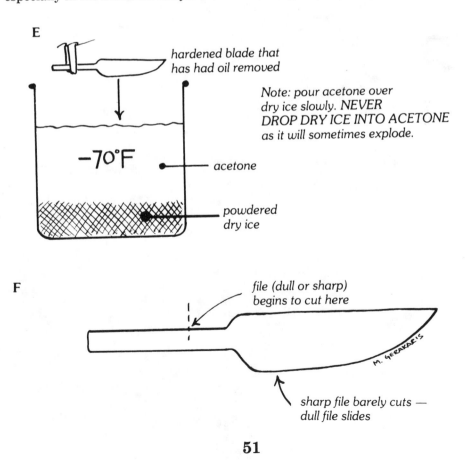

E

hardened blade that
has had oil removed

Note: pour acetone over
dry ice slowly. NEVER
DROP DRY ICE INTO ACETONE
as it will sometimes explode.

−70°F

acetone

powdered
dry ice

F

file (dull or sharp)
begins to cut here

M. GERAKAMS

sharp file barely cuts —
dull file slides

51

Secrets of Successful Tempering

1. Put a 1/4" to 3/8" mild steel plate over the fire and temper blades on this plate. (See photo). Control temperature carefully by heating the plate. Never heat the blade in an open flame (it changes too fast). Group I changes hardness levels fast, so watch carefully. Groups II and III take longer to temper. When tempering at high temperatures, use a heated bar and quench to stop tempering action. Double edge blades should lay flat and be watched carefully as they tend to change fast.

2. Keep blade in constant motion on the plate, occasionally laying the guard area of the tang on the plate to insure stress relief in this critical area. The approximate time is 5 to 20 minutes. Note: L-6, A-2, D-2, M-2, 154CM and 440C will become harder after second tempering.

3. Use dull and sharp files interchangeably around the silhouette to judge the degree of softening. This step is very sensitive and requires a lot of practice.

4. Test toughness of the blade by striking it across something such as a cutoff hardy.

Note: Hardening and tempering steps are not difficult to accomplish in a

manual way, but require much practice to acquire the sensitivity necessary to distinquish very subtle differences in hardness and softness levels using dull and sharp files.

This concludes the part which has stressed the bladesmith's relationship to new materials using old techniques. The most helpful suggestion that I can think of, centers on the awareness of the smith to the material. In a way, this material is very fragile and will burn or crack if treated severely. On the other hand, if worked slowly and with much attention to small details, these new materials can be shaped into strong, tough shapes that function as well as they look.

The Finishing Room

In one corner of great granddad's shop was a space with a wooden floor. In this area on long benches, were various hand tools and hand powered machines for drilling and grinding. Others were run with a foot treadle like a sewing machine. On the bench a wide variety of jigs used to guide one tool in the making of another, e.g., files, were made from annealed tool steel by scribing them in a jig that locked the bar in place while a hardened wedge shaped cutter was pulled across it.

A long rack up near the ceiling held oak and hickory rods used for handle material. Occasionally cow bone, horn and deer antler were used for knife handles.

The work in this corner was very time consuming and required long hours of concentration in order to attain the necessary skills. This is the area where my father learned the value of filing a straight line in iron or steel. Here was a place where habits were developed at a young age that allowed the craftsman to develop his or her artistic talent. I have watched my father use hand operated or cranked machines with more precision than one run by electrical power.

A walk into my shop today provides a view similar to the shop that my father worked in. The large bench I use was his along with most of the hand tools. I also have some of his electrical equipment including two grinders, a drill press and sander.

The tools that I use are not unusual and can be found in most garage type shops. I no longer make my own files nor for that matter do I use hand cranked machines with the exception of the forge. But in spite of the use of some modern tools, most of the work is still done by hand.

My finishing room is an area where the jobs started on the forge are completed. The knife blades that have a crude shape are silhouetted, shaped, sanded smooth, drilled or threaded and sent back to be hardened and tempered. Afterwards, the blades are ground and sanded in preparation for the hilts.

The many woods in addition to hickory and oak are still end grain sealed and stored high in one corner near the ceiling. Antler and cow horn are cleaned, hollowed and stored in cans for curing. A wide variety of brass, bronze, and nickel silver is stored for shaping into guards and pommels.

Perhaps the items that have changed the most between then and now, besides the steel, are the abrasives. Previously, one used various abrasive powders of different grits sprinkled on leather coated with glue. The leather was then fastened to wooden wheels and used to smooth and polish the steel and wood. Now, the abrasive not only comes fixed to the paper or cloth, but new materials like silicon carbide have joined the list of traditional ones like corundum (alumina- aluminum oxide) and crocus of iron. The use of buffing compounds has likewise expanded.

What follows is a list of the various tools and machines which I use in the construction of a knife with a brief description of how I use them: a 1/2

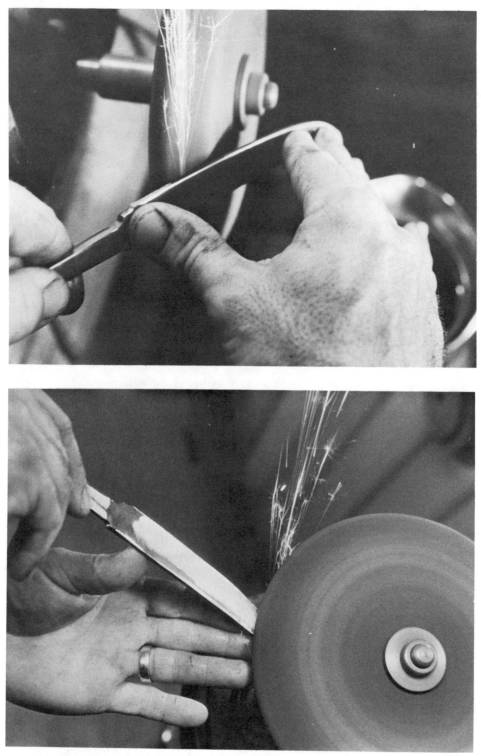

horsepower, high speed 1"x7" grinder and wheel dresser. This tool is used twice in the operation, once to shape, i.e., silhouette, the knife and, after heat treating, to thin and shape the blade and tang; a 1/3 horsepower motor mounted with a 9" V shaped wheel for hollow or concave grinding; a 1/2 horsepower motor mounted with buffer and cut off wheel (steel); a 1/3 horsepower side wheel, 4" sanding disc used to flatten steel and wood; a 1/3 horsepower motor connected by a pulley to a soft 2-1/2x 18-15/16" rubber wheel (Hy-Pol) available in lapidary and jewerly supply stores. This small, inexpensive wheel fitted with sleeve sanding belts is a most useful tool. With 36 grit belts I can grind; with finer grit belts (120-600 grit), I can smooth and polish; 3 electric hand drills: one is small and high speed. These tools are used to drill both steel and wood. The small drill is fitted with cratex wheels for removing scratches. Cratex (trade name) is rubber that has been impregnated with abrasives; an oxyacetylene (or oxypropane) torch fitted with microsize tips. I use this apparatus for soldering on the guards with low melt, All State stainless steel solder (paste and wire type) No.430 (Note: Read instructions for use carefully before using oxyacetylene); several steel block heat sinks plus clamps. Heat sinks absorb and dissipate heat in this case, away from the knife blade and tang. Note: Propane is cheaper than acetylene and burns cleaner. Duzall flux is very important with No.430 solder. I even used it with the paste solder that already has a flux with it. Yellow ochre powder is mixed with water to control the flow of the solder (produced by Dixon Co. and available at craft supply stores); flat, precision ground steel plates- 1" thick 12"x12" for flattening wood to bone, brass to steel, etc; files 4" to 6" open cut, engineering type; fine, smooth precision files have a tendency to clog and are unsatisfactory for my work; buffing wheels and buffing compound, i.e. stainless, emery, tripol and 180-400 grit greaseless buffing compounds to remove small scratches from the finished blade. (Greaseless buffing compounds are available from a variety of knife finishing supply companies. It is important to keep the wheels separate for each compound. NuLife abrasive belt cleaner is an art gum type of material that is excellent for cleaning sandpaper and abrasive belts which helps prevent overheating of the material (available from local distributers of the Abrasive Service Co. Inc., PO Box 128, 56 New Britain Ave., Unionville, CT 06085); three step finish for use on bone, wood, antler, ivory. I have used this material with very good results on a variety of materials. It helps waterproof the handle and prevents expansion and contraction of the tight fitting joints. It includes sealer, wax, and finish (made by General Finishes, 1580 S. 81st, Milwaukee, WI 53214); assorted hammers, punches, feeler gauges, scribes (for metal); glues- Epoxy, household type, rubber cement, cement for gluing sandpaper discs to side wheel sander (Feathering Disc Adhesive); sandpapers- I use a wide variety of aluminum oxide and silicon carbide type papers available in most hardware stores; hardwoods-(See USDA Forest Service Research paper FPL 125 Mar 1970. Material for leather and sharpening are listed in these sections); *Safety Equipment and Practice,* Forest Products Lab, Madison, WI. Goggles and a safety shield are very important for eye protection as are ear plugs (f requently sold in hardware stores and tool stores) and disposable masks and cartridge type safety masks. My work area is small and easy to control with plenty of windows for venting fumes and cleaning. Modern chemicals and electricity are the source of most hazardous conditions in my shop. Aside from electrical machines with moving parts, other unexpected dangers arise in the shop. Steel particles accumulating in electrical plugs can cause fires.

57

Knife Finishing Procedures

What follows is a description of the steps that I take to convert a relatively shapeless blade blank into a finished knife. I will give the general procedures used so that the reader will have a preview of the steps before the necessary details are supplied.

The forged blade blank is silhouetted to the shape of the finished knife. The blade is then sanded on either side to the desired thickness. Any filing, drilling or threading is done before the blade is hardened and tempered. After the blade is heat treated, the final shaping and polishing is done. Next, the guard material is selected, measured, tapped and/or drilled. The guard is slipped over the tang and made flush with the blade. The guard is soldered in place and the excess solder is scraped and sanded off. The handle material is measured, sanded flat, drilled and slipped over the tang. If the knife has a metal pommel, the brass or bronze etc. is measured, flattened, tapped and threaded. All of the pieces are assembled, shaped, glued, and put into a press to set. When dry, the hilt is sanded to the final shape and the last step is to put on the three finishing coats.

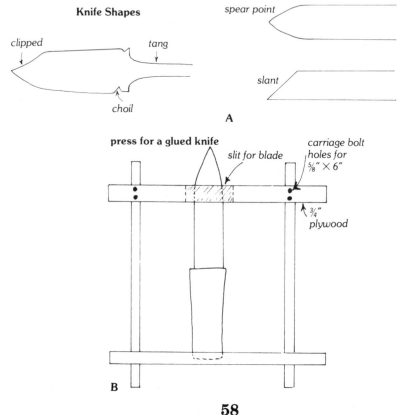

Knife Shapes

spear point

clipped

tang

slant

choil

A

press for a glued knife

slit for blade

carriage bolt
holes for
$\frac{5}{8}'' \times 6''$

$\frac{3}{4}''$
plywood

B

Along with the mechanical steps, I will include both my design and aesthetic approach to this art form. I would also like to emphasize that the methods, tools, etc. that I employ, may not exactly fit someone else; this description fits my style and perhaps may be employed by anyone with the desire to try the techniques.

My idea of a knife is that it is an extension of the hand; as such it should be comfortable to hold. I draw many of the shapes that I use from forms such as birds and fish which display to me both balance and grace. It is one thing to visualize these shapes but quite another to combine them into a durable art object that will stand up under everyday use.

I prefer, in most cases, to look for the simplest solutions to knife making that satisfy me. For example, knife balance is comfort in use. The hilt should be so contructed that you feel that your hand has an extension which is cutting. Therefore, the shape of the knife is the most important thing to me. Each blade shape is contoured for ease of function. Any sharp blade will cut, but some shapes cut with less effort. By the same token, for every blade shape, there is an ideal handle to match. The trick is to be able to find that combination.

I believe there are no hard and fast rules for the construction of a knife. Whatever works is what is best for any particular situation. Through long experience, I have learned to follow certain patterns.

Regardless of the blade length, the tang must be at least as long as the palm of the hand is wide, and perferably longer. This usually means from 3-1/2" to over 4" long. The only exceptions that I encounter are short bladed knives with blades 2-1/2" and smaller. The hilt must have support throughout its length. My hilts run from 4-1/2" to 5" long and the tangs vary from 4" to 4-1/2" long.

The junction of the blade and tang is a weak spot in a knife (Diag.C). I widen and thicken this area to protect it against the stress of a lifetime of use. Square corner filings are to be avoided when possible because they are stress points. Thus, round off sharp edges when encountered in shaping the tang. As the knife design calls for a wider or longer blade, so, also, the junction of blade to tang must widen and thicken to accommodate this change.

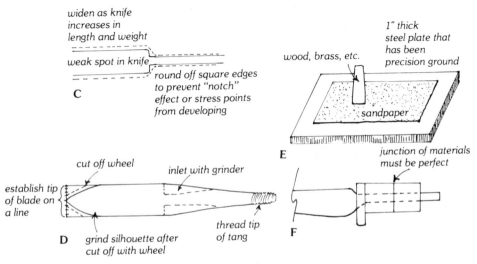

widen as knife
increases in
length and weight

weak spot in knife

round off square edges
to prevent "notch"
effect or stress points
from developing

C

1" thick
steel plate that
has been
precision ground

wood, brass, etc.

sandpaper

E

junction of materials
must be perfect

cut off wheel

inlet with grinder

establish tip
of blade on
a line

thread tip
of tang

D   grind silhouette after
cut off with wheel

F

Of the many other details to be discussed, the most important concerns the fitting of the many joints. Where one piece of material meets another, that area must show the closest possible fitting. The time spent in achieving this tight fit is sometimes great. I spend much time on this both to strengthen the piece and preserve the flow patterns.

I start the blade design by sketching the silhouette on the forged blank (Diag.D). I use the grinder and cut off wheel to do the shaping. Even though the blade has not been heat treated, it can be damaged by grinding too hard. Now the sides can be smoothed to a uniform thickness (1/8" or thinner). Once the scale has been removed on the sides, I determine what style of blade contour that I want. This varies from flat sided to concave with many contours in between (Note: the blade has enough metal along the edge to thin down after it has been hardened). Regardless of whether or not the blade is flat or concave, it should ultimately be thin near the edge, as thin blades cut far more efficiently than thick ones.

Adjust the side thickness so that the area where the guard will be has flat parallel sides. This area will be the thickest part of the knife. The guard slips over the tang and fits evenly to the blade. I use the guard size and shape to balance the whole knife. For small, light knives, the guard may be 1/8" thick. At the other extreme, the guard may reach 3/4" thickness. I also use thin guards to accentuate the handle material. Heavy guards bring added weight to a heavy knife that may be used for chopping.

The design possibilities for the handle have been drastically altered with the advent of modern glues. This material is not perfect however. I have found that epoxy loses its strength when exposed over a long period of time to the air. To minimize the exposure of the glue, I try to eliminate it from all joints. In this way the epoxy will serve the purpose for which it is designed–to hold– without shrinking away from the tang. Do not use epoxy to secure the guard because, after much experimenting, I have found that solder is stronger and longer lasting.

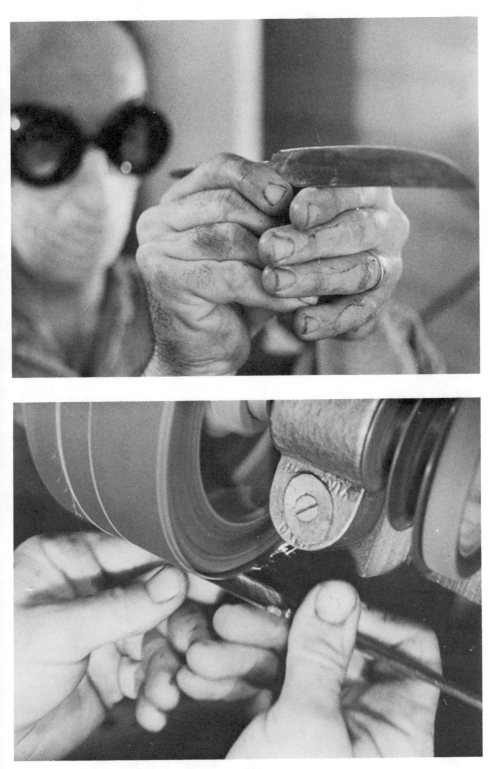

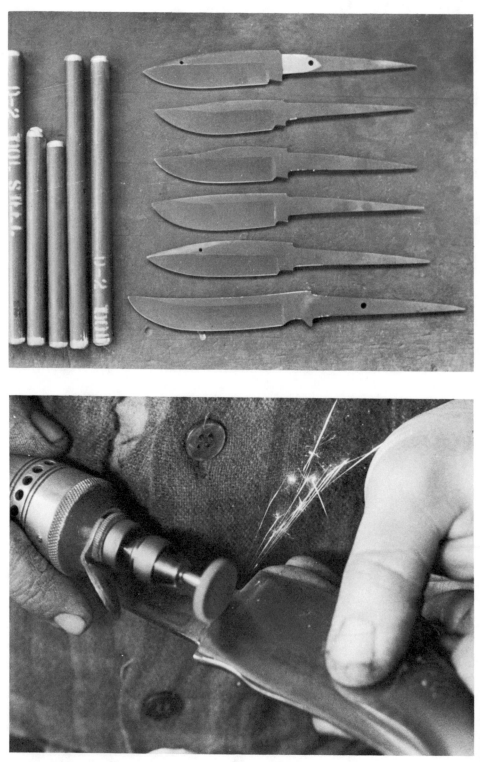

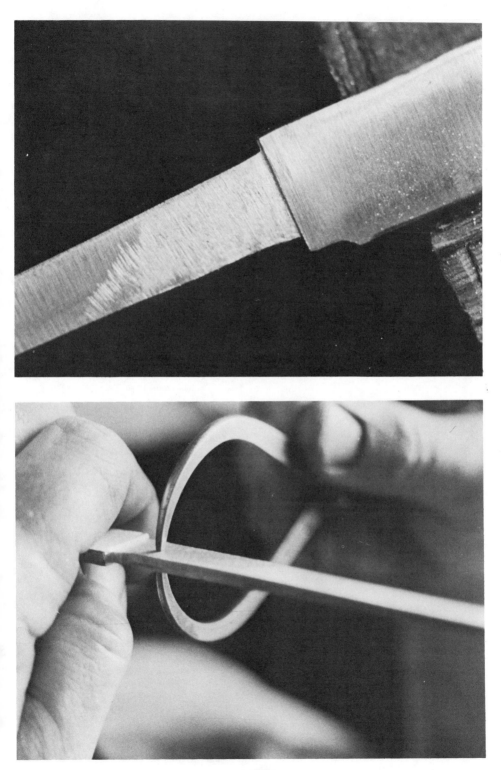

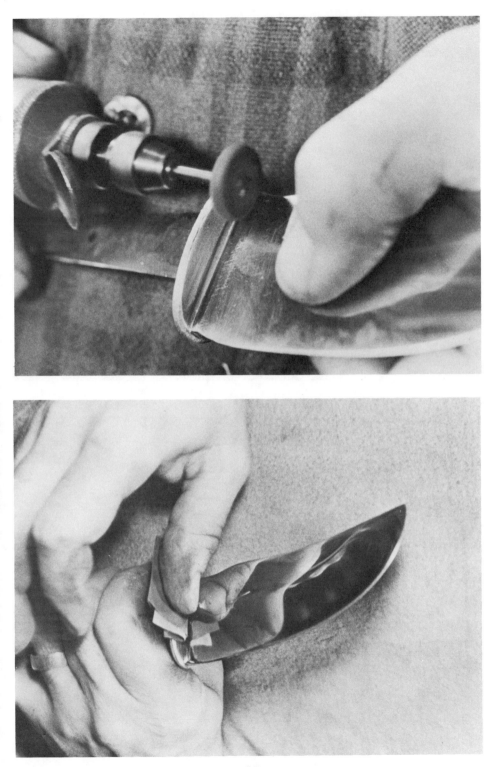

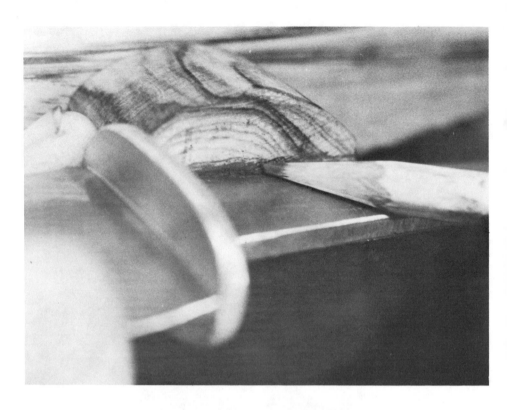

70

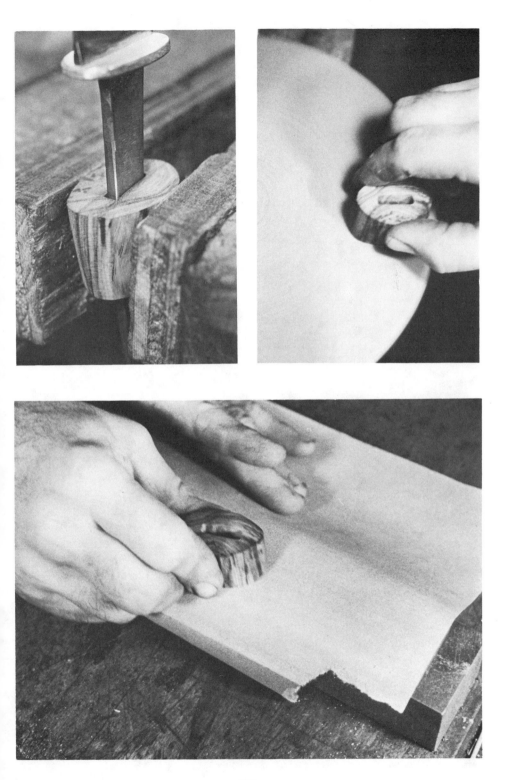

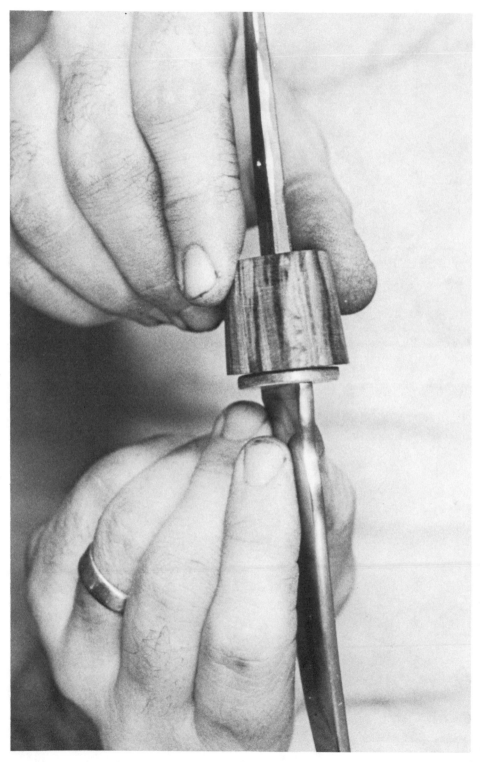

Threading and Drilling
The Tang

In addition to epoxy, I use two methods for attaching the handle. The simplest involves drilling one or more holes in the tang and the handle material which is in turn held in place by a pin made of goat horn or cow horn.

The other method is to thread a piece of brass, bronze, or nickel silver to the end of the tang (Diag. D). I first thread the tang tip using a threading tool while the tang is soft (annealed). Frequently, the tip of the tang is too hard to thread and requires re-annealing. A matching threaded hole is put into the pommel.

If this style handle is used, I make the guard and pommel first and then fit the handle material in between the two.

Handle Material

I have found that there is a wide variety of acceptable natural materials that can be used for making handles. I select materials that by their nature will not shrink to any great degree. All natural materials, e.g., wood, antler, bone, ivory, and even very dense equatorial hardwoods, contain small amounts of water. I therefore use kiln dried wood and aged antler, bone, etc. I generally keep newly acquired material one year or more before using.

The next requirement is wear resistance and toughness. Many hardwoods fit these requirements very well, e.g., cocobolo, pau (Brazilian ironwood), wenge, Brazilian rosewood and many more.

I have learned to stay away from less dense woods like maple, walnut and zebrawood etc., because they are not as wear resistant as the ones listed above. If you can press your fingernail into the wood, then it is too soft, regardless of its looks. It may also be more porous and expand and contract on becoming wet and consequently dry out.

I enjoy combining various woods so they will be both pleasing and durable. For example, I select one to two inches of a dense wood, like cocobolo, and secure it adjacent to the guard. Then I fit the remainder of the handle with goncalo alves. Or instead of wood near the guard, I sometimes substitute another material. I try to butt the most dense material near the guard where the fingers squeeze and wear the handle. Even ebony, which has a tendency to crack in large sections, may be safely used in this area.

When working with these materials, work them slowly so that they will not overheat. I sand with an open cutting sandpaper. I usually start with a 36 grit paper and work to 80 grit. When the crude shape is established, I concentrate on assembling all of the parts making sure that they fit perfectly together. Having a large flat surface upon which to sand makes all the difference in the world (Diag. E). Note: The most important skills to develop with wood in making handles is learning to drill straight, narrowly defined holes that match the tang shape, and proper holding positions for the wood when pushing it across the sandpaper in order to make it perfectly flat.

Woods that have open grain types like oak, wenge, hickory etc., require special handling because of their tendency to splinter. I rasp or sand across the grain very slowly when shaping and after the finish sanding, apply generous sealers to the surface to seal the wide open pores.

Antler is an excellent handle material. It is a connective tissue outgrowth of the skull which subsequently becomes calcified bone. The core of the antler is spongy material with blood vessels which furnish calcium and nutrients to the antler.

The bone of the antler is thicker near the skull and is thus more desirable for handles. I judge antlers on both the length toward the tip of this thick portion and how well this material has been preserved. The most desirable racks that I have used have been stored inside for long periods of time and have dried out slowly. I avoid antlers that have been outside too long and have either cracked or decalcified.

Hollowing out the dry spongy material must be done with great care so that

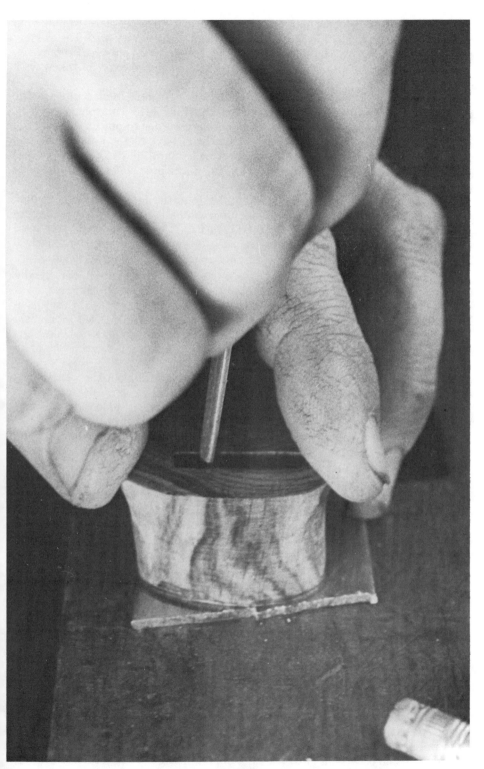

the hard bone does not become too thin. The most difficult place to hollow is the area adjacent to the button. I start hollowing the cavity with the electric drill and finish with a series of gouges and long, thin wood chisels. I remove as much of the spongy material as I can, so that the space may be taken with epoxy glue.

If the antler is thick, it gives you the chance to mold and sculpture the material in many ways. If patiently sanded, the finish is like marble.

I sometimes drill the tang and antler or wood in order to put a retaining pin in place. This operation requires lots of practice. I have tested knives with and without the pin and found no difference as far as durability is concerned. The determining factor of handle longevity, I feel, is the preciseness of the fittings and the quality of the glue (Diag. F).

Another material that is somewhat similar to antler is ivory. Ivory is much denser and harder than antler and bone. I occasionally use ivory in the place of antler. It is very hard but can be brittle, so I only use it in small sections. I sand ivory with great care since it has a tendency to surface check if overheated. In fact, heat or direct sunlight can cause this material to crack.

Very old ivory, or fossil ivory, is also used to some extent for handle material. Fossil ivory is very hard material that has, through the ages, been changed by the continued deposition of minerals into the ivory. These fossil ivories come from walrus tusk, walrus tooth, Mammoth and Mastodon tusk. This material is found in the Arctic coastal and interior regions of Alaska. The color of fossil ivory ranges from a creamy white, through a carmel color to almost black.

Fossil ivory is a very desirable material for the scrimshaw artist. According to scrimshander, Steve Magill, Scrimshaw is derived from the latin word "scribe" which means to write or make pictures. Scrimshaw also includes carvings and adornments some of which date back 25,000 years to the caves of France. There, beautiful artifacts have been found made of mammoth and mastodon ivory. These were carved by Cro-Magnon man.

During the 18th and 19th centuries, American scrimshaw has been associated with the whaling industry. In fact, it is a true American folk art that can be seen at the Whaling Museum in Sharon, Massachusetts, on page 131 and 132 of this book, and many other places.

Up to this point, I have described the construction of knives with narrow tangs that are surrounded by the hilt. Since I prefer this style, I have emphasized it. The full tang knife handle design has a tang that is a silhouette of its final shape in steel. The handle consists of slabs of material attached to either side of the tang. The handle is attached with pins that pass through the tang and handle.

When I forge this type of knife, I cut the steel to the desired length, silhouette the tang and forge out the blade. (Note: stock lengthening depends on the original width, i.e., 3/16" goes to 1/8" width, with an increase of about 2" in length.) I next grind the blade shape that I desire and drill holes in the tang for the guard and handle. Never use an oxyacetylene torch to cut out the steel, as it will completely destroy the steel for an unknown distance from the cut.

I secure the guard with two pins which are clamped tightly and soldered in place. Next, the wood or antler is fitted. An easy method of securing the slabs is to first glue one side, drill through the handle material and tang when dry and glue on the other side. Put the pins in last, being very careful not to injure the wood. Be sure the pins are the same size as the holes that you drill.

Whatever type of natural material I use, the requirements are the same, a combination of strength, texture, workability and beauty. There is no reason to sacrifice strength when selecting natural materials. The thing about natural materials that has always appealed to me is their wide variety of textures and colors. Even in the same piece of wood, there can be amazing difference. These small differences may be used to create subtle differences in the hilt.

The use of the various combinations of hilt materials is a matter of taste. The development of that taste takes time and patience and is not something that can be acquired overnight or by someone trying to explain it. I have found that the mechanical steps only become easier through continuous practice. Each step in making a knife is critical to me so that any error made can only be made worse by continued work. I am in no rush to make the knife as I happen to feel that the only way that I can create what I want is by slow, deliberate and patient steps; always remaining centered on the image of what I would like to create. Many times I am surprised at the results and have to get used to the object that I created because it does not fit the image that I had. So be it.

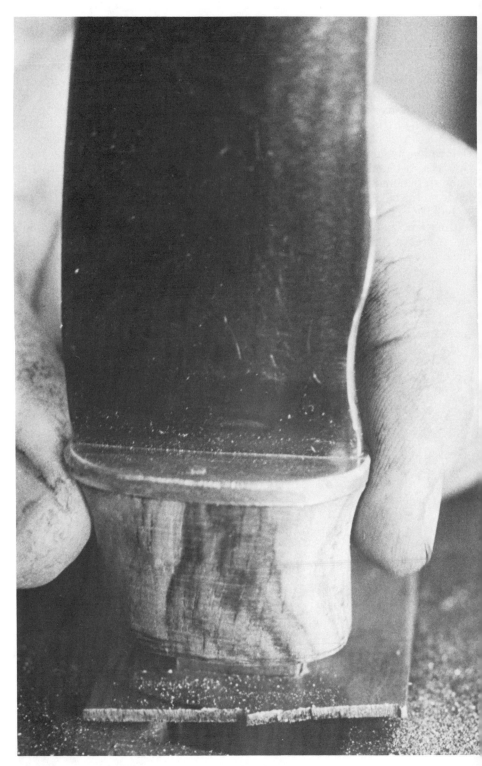

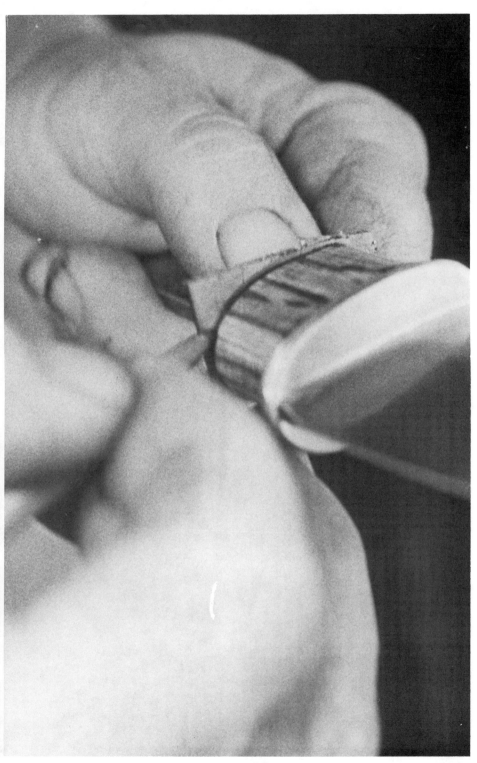

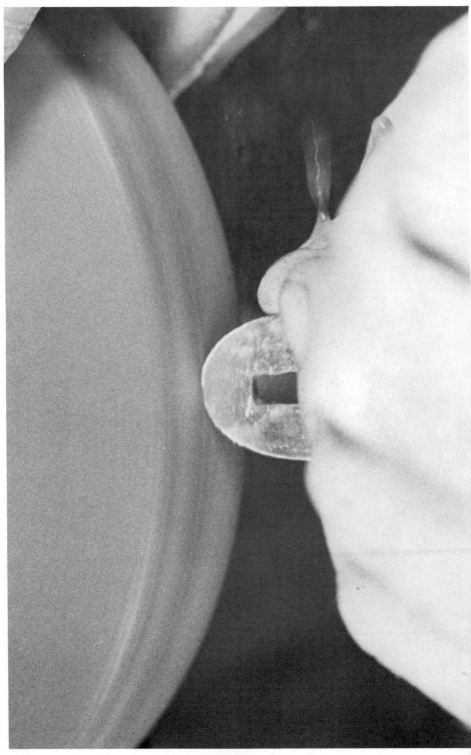

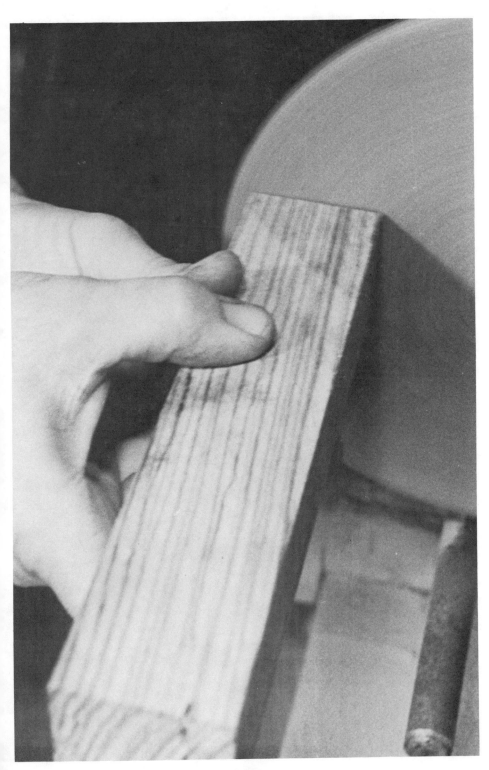

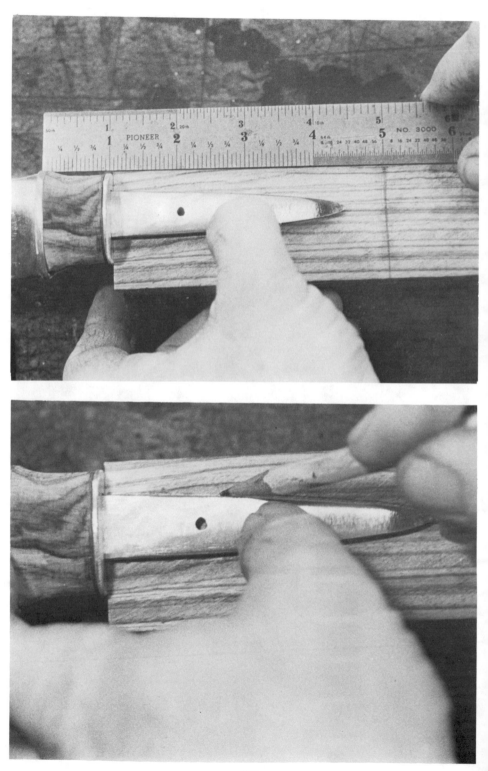

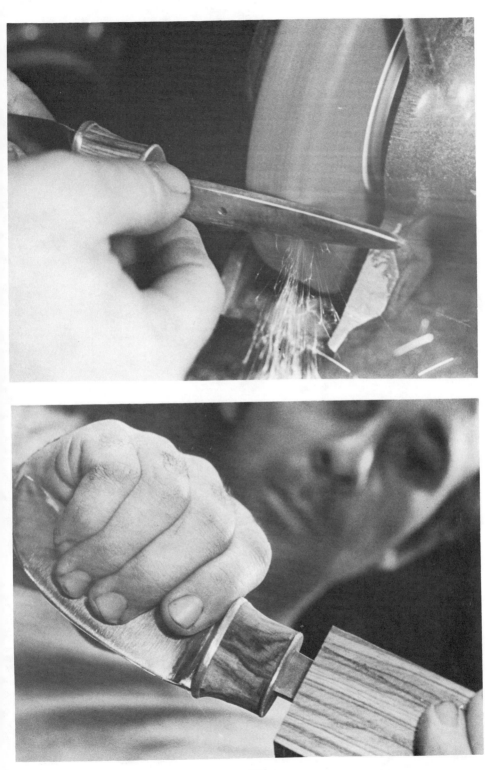

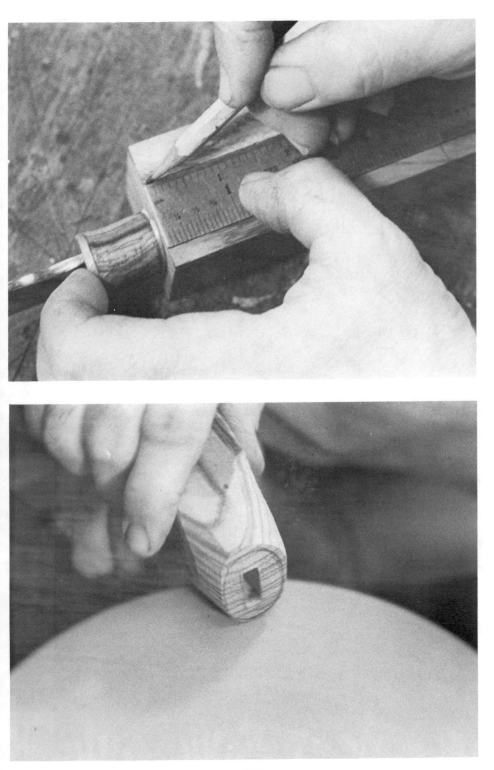

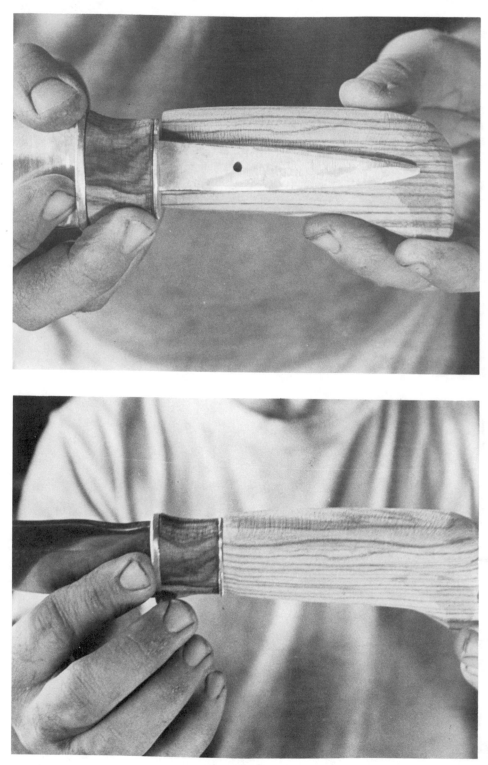

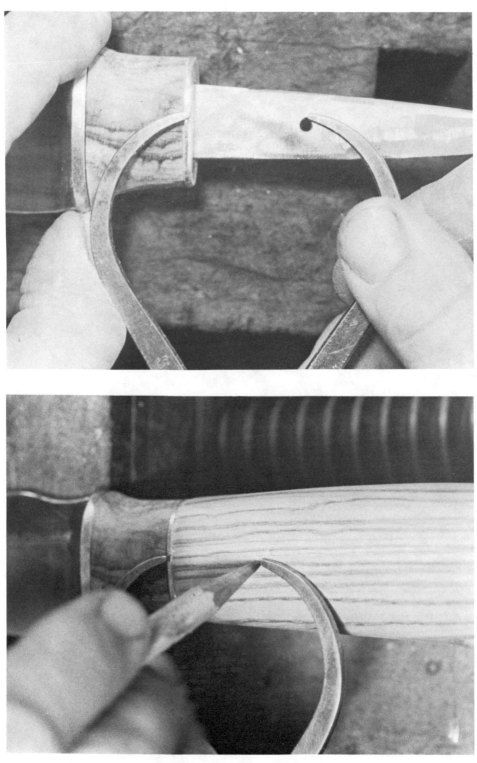

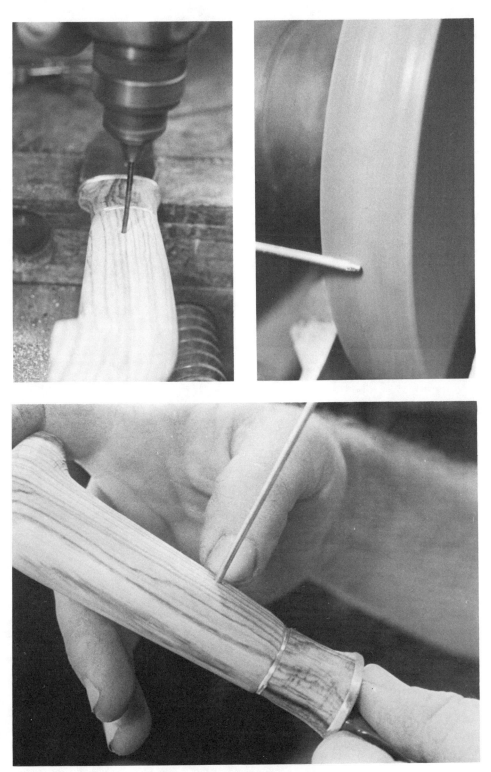

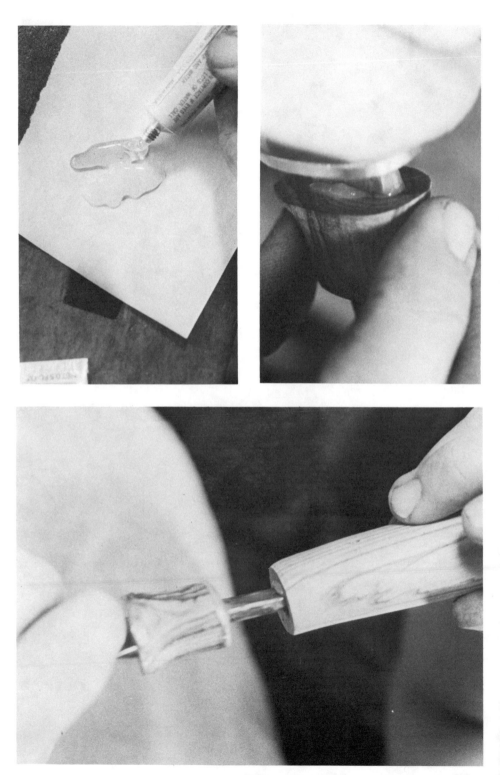

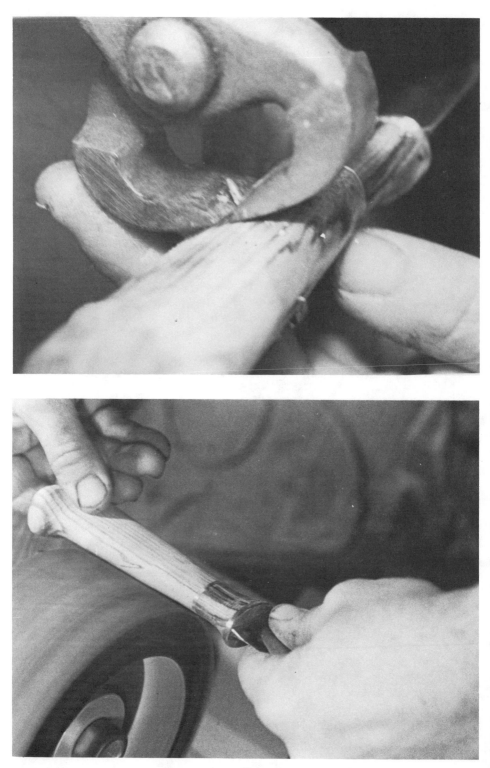

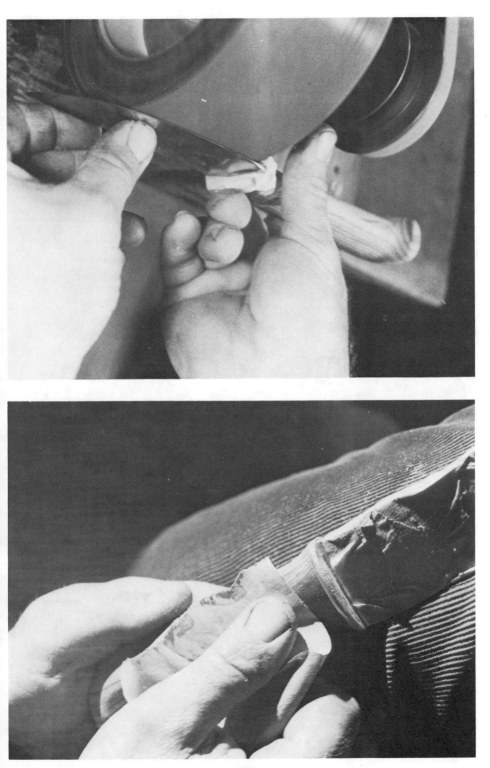

The Hand Stitched Leather Sheath

Most of the knives that I make are meant to be used. Since I constantly find an every day use for a knife, I have over the years experimented with different types of sheaths in which to carry a knife. The criteria that I have used include: simple design, no breakable snaps, strong construction and a durable non stretch belt attachment. The resulting sheath meets this set of objectives for most knives that I make.

The sheath is a type of pouch with the leather covering not only the blade but three quarters of the hilt. The knife is thus protected by an envelope of leather.

I start the sheath by first selecting a piece of 9-10 ounce oak tanned cow hide (unstained) and, laying the knife on its left side, draw with a pencil, a line on the rough side of the leather along the edge of the knife and then extend the line away from the back of the edge. This makes a flap of leather wide enough to fold over the knife.

This piece of leather is cut out and laid down with the knife in position to make a spacer. This thread protecting spacer is made of heavy sole leather. The silhouette of the blade is drawn on the sole leather (which also extends up the hilt). Next, the sole leather is cut on the silhouetted line and then, allowing for the stitching, cut out. This piece of heavy leather is glued, with rubber cement, to the rough side of the leather. Holes are drilled with a drill press along a line evenly from where the point of the knife will be to the top. Fit the size of the hole to the size of the pre-waxed stitching thread to be used.

Next, the belt attachment is made. This holdfast is made of three parts. The two smaller sections are to be drilled and stitched to the sheath. (Note: Drill from the rough side). The middle section which extends over the other two is cut, glued on to the others, smoothed with the sanding wheel, stained on the sides and waxed with carbowax used in shoe repair shops. The three piece unit is made flush with the top edge of the sheath. Then, with a pointed marker, the sheath is marked for drilling. Note: The sides of the three piece attachment are parallel with the holes previously drilled in the sheath. Now the sheath is lightly stained with a cream stain combo leather conditioner. (I do not like most stains since they tend to cover the grain of the leather).

The stitching must be sunken into the leather in order to preserve the thread. I wet the parts to be stitched with warm water and, using a leather tool, groove the leather where the stitching is to run. (Note: it is important to groove the area which will be on the opposite side of the belt attachment.)

I next stitch the belt holder to the sheath. This belt holder has a built in gap to accommodate the belt and does not have a tendency to pull or stretch out of shape.

I hand stitch the leather using a heavy pre-waxed leather thread. The leather is very heavy so I use a pair of pliers to pull the thread through the holes. Note: the needles used are heavy duty leather needles. The type of stitch that I use has a needle at either end of the thread so that both sides of the sheath are stit-

97

ched at the same time.

When the belt holder is in place, the inside of the sheath is wet with warm water and, with the knife in place, the leather is molded over the knife. The knife is then removed and holes are drilled through the ones drilled before. After the stitching is completed, the knife is inserted onto the sheath and molded once more.

The sheath is completed by sanding the edge, staining it and waxing the sides. I apply a liquid wax to the sheath and let it dry for 2 to 3 days. After the sheath is thoroughly dry, I put two coats of shoe polish on it.

List of Tools Used
in Sheath Making

★ 9-10 oz. Oak Tanned tooling leather
★ Leather rubber cement
★ Heavy duty leather needles
★ Groover
★ Pliers
★ Cream brown stain (antique stain)
★ Brown dye
★ Drill press
★ Waxed thread (heavy duty)
★ Carbo Hard Wax (brown)
★ Atom liquid Wax

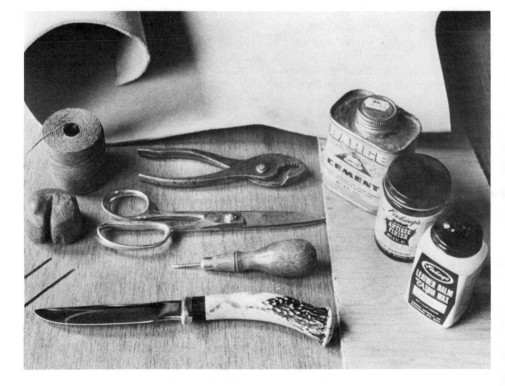

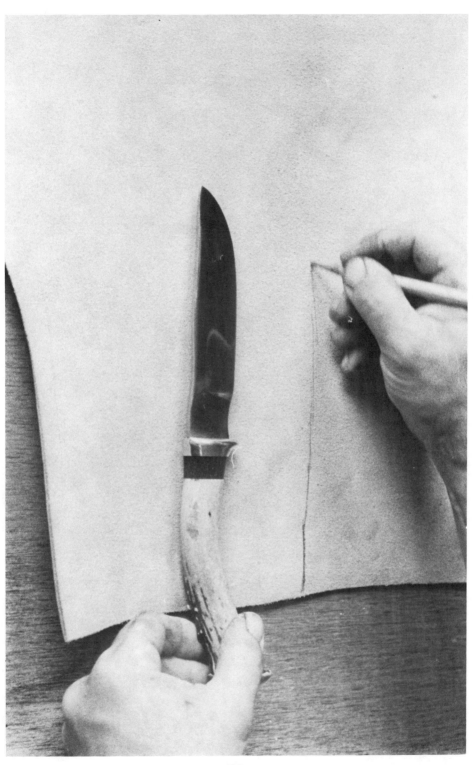

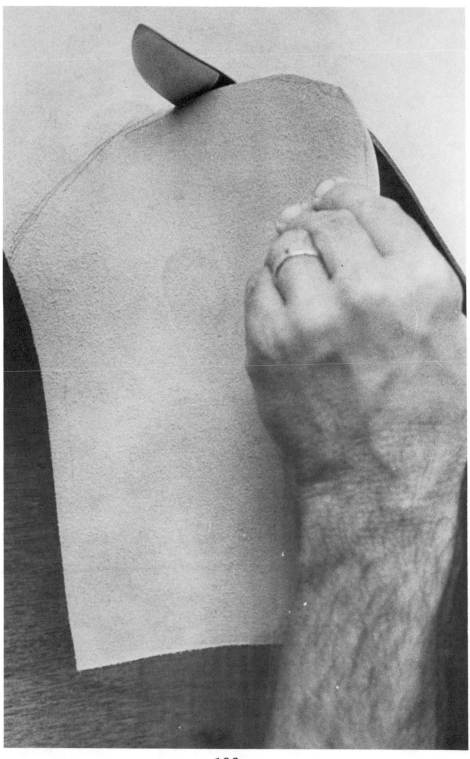

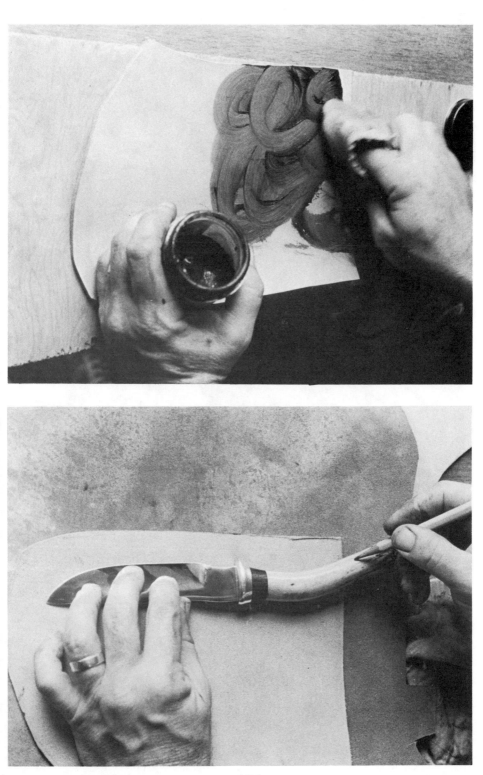

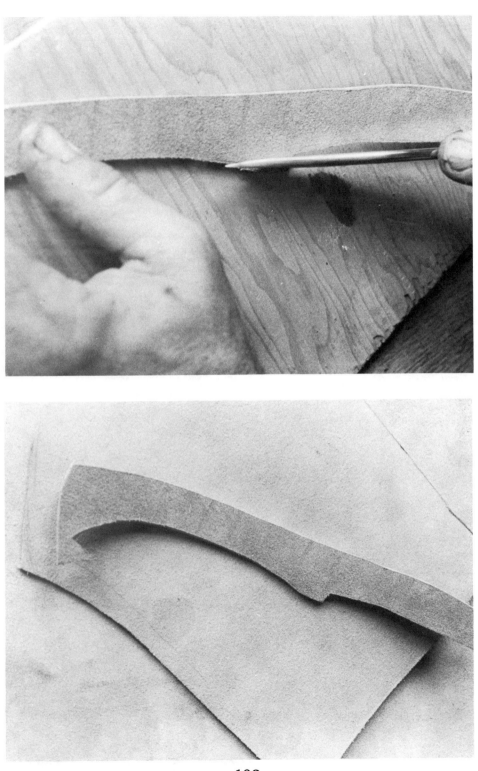

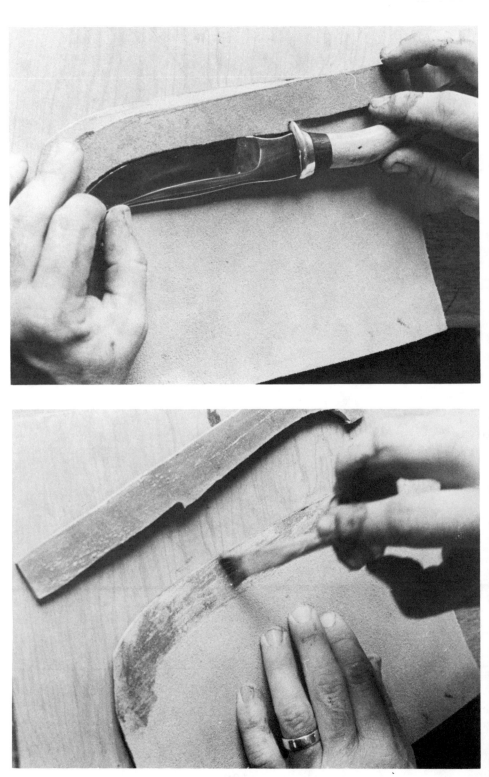

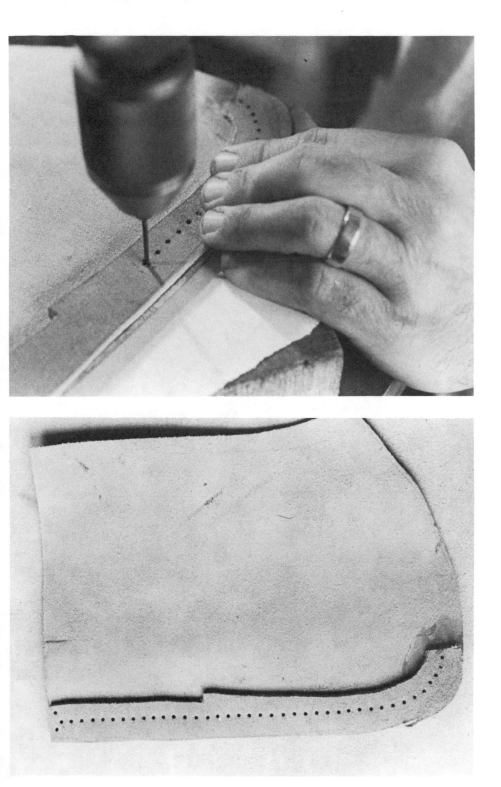

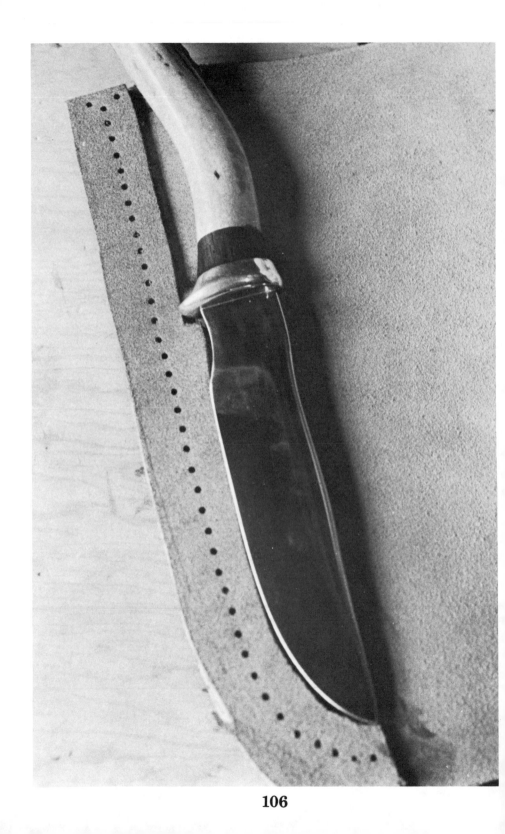

106

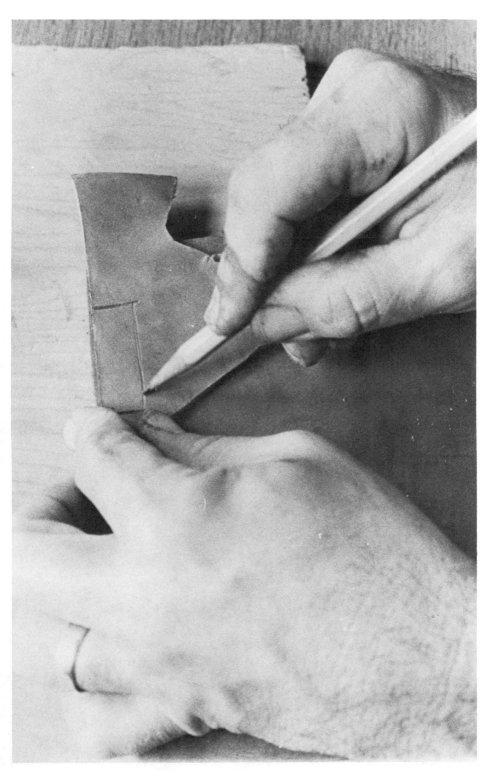

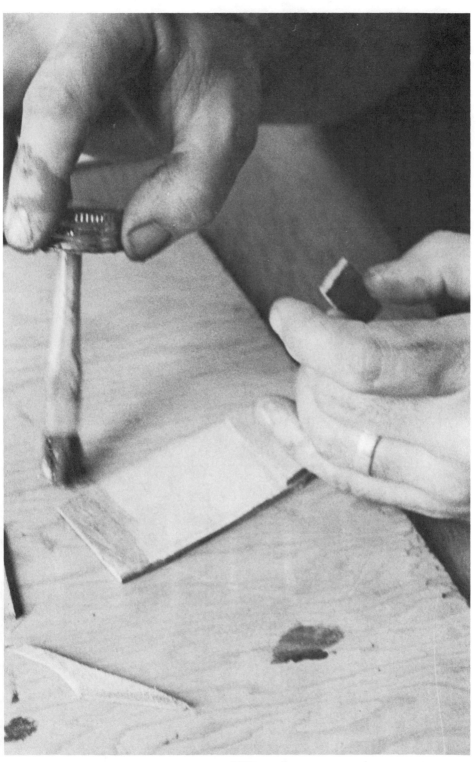

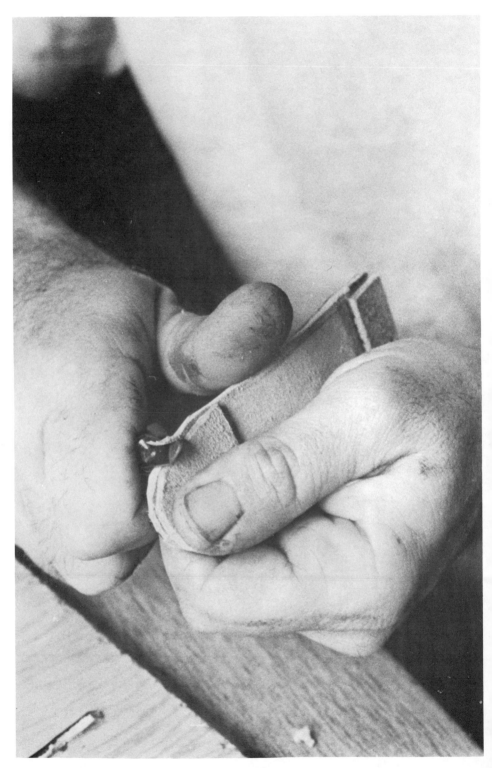

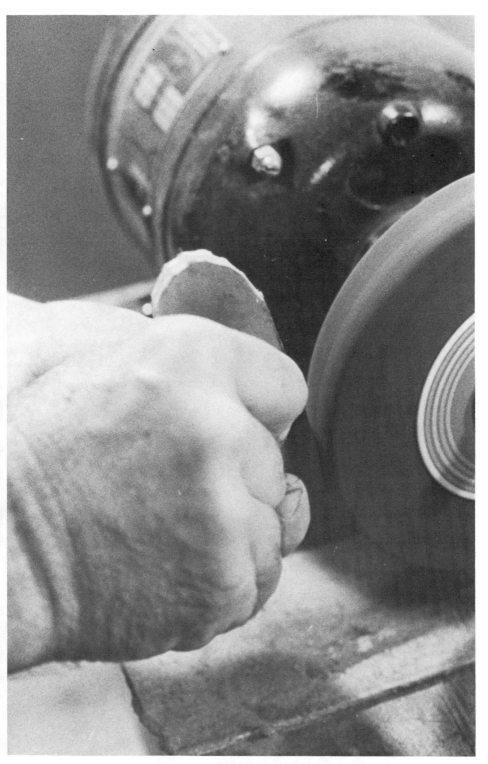

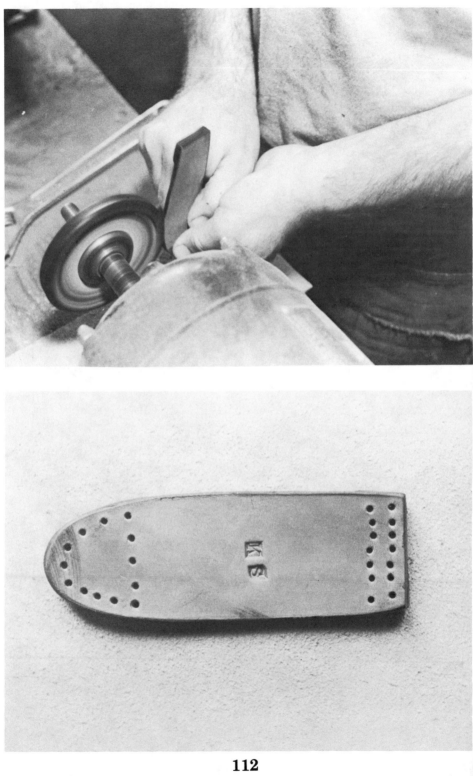

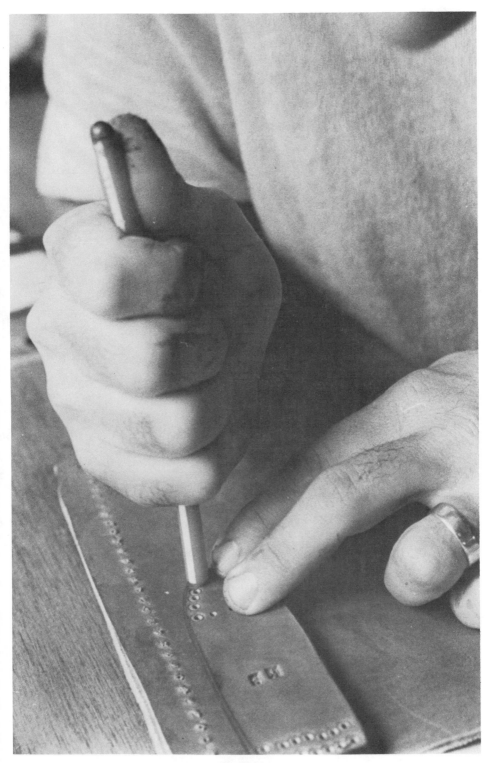

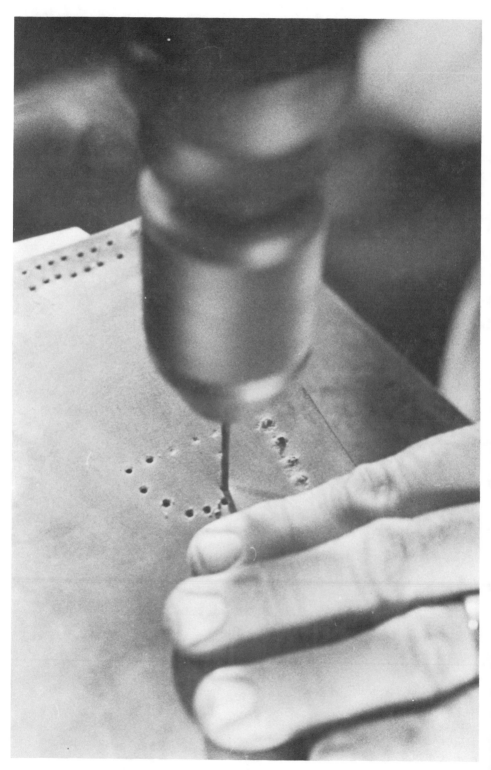

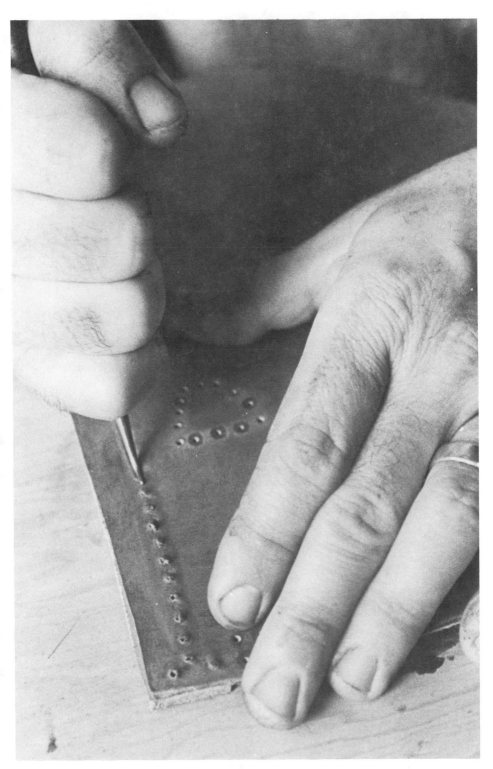

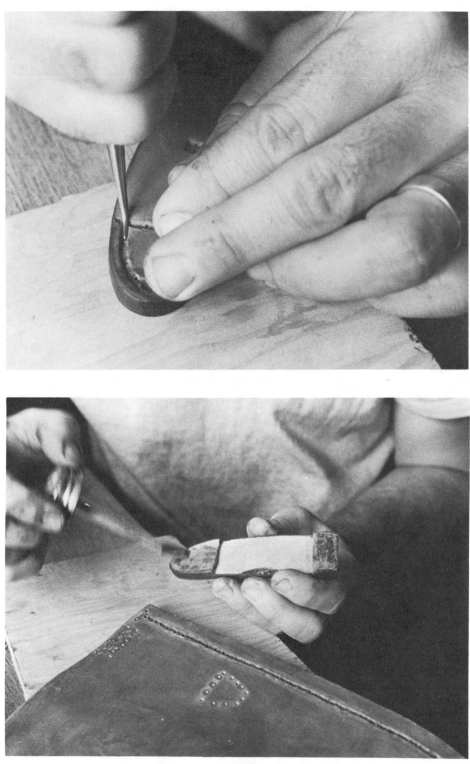

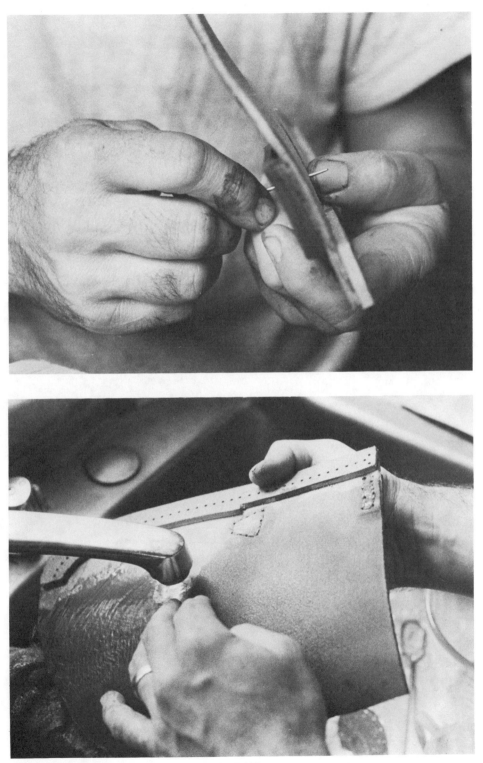

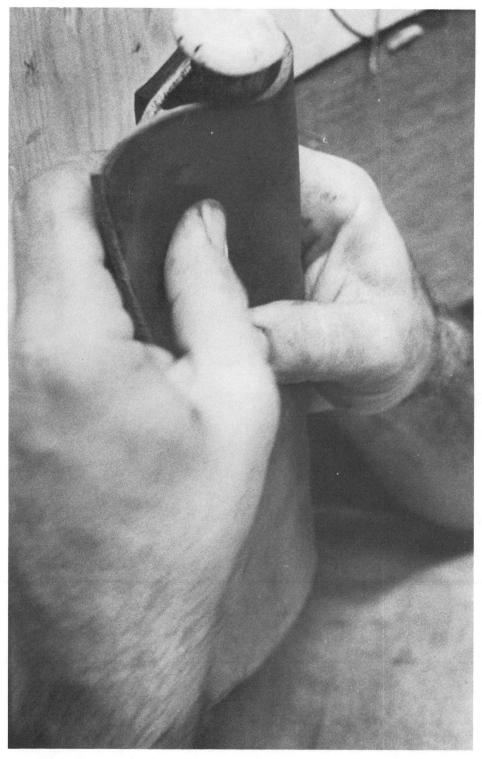

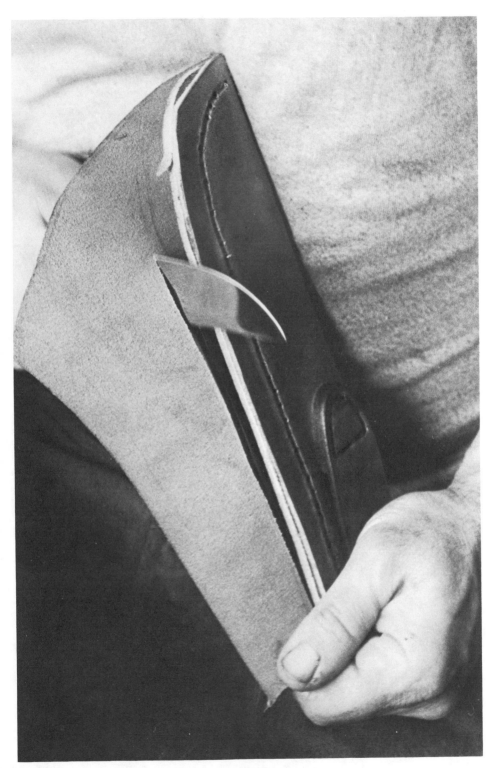

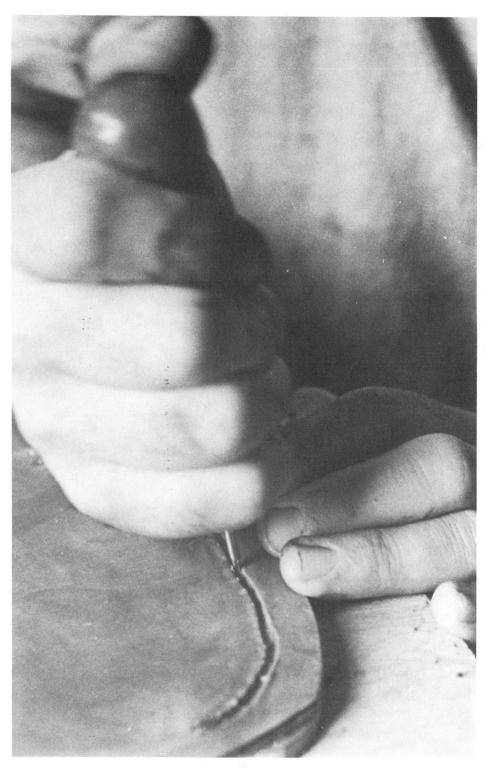

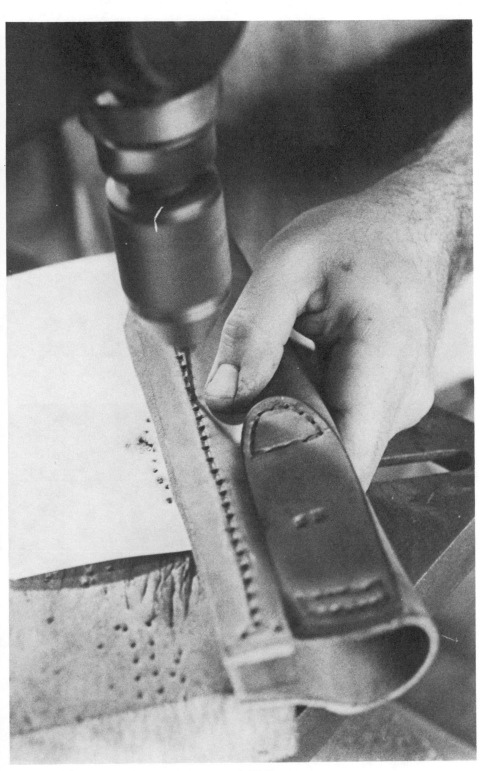

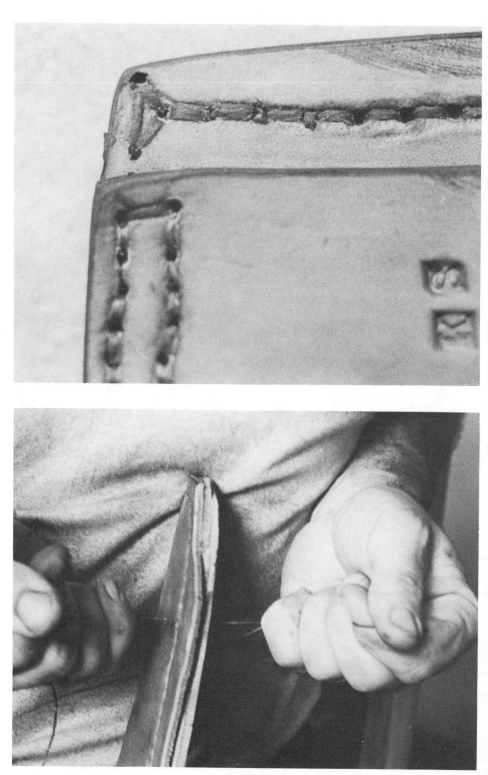

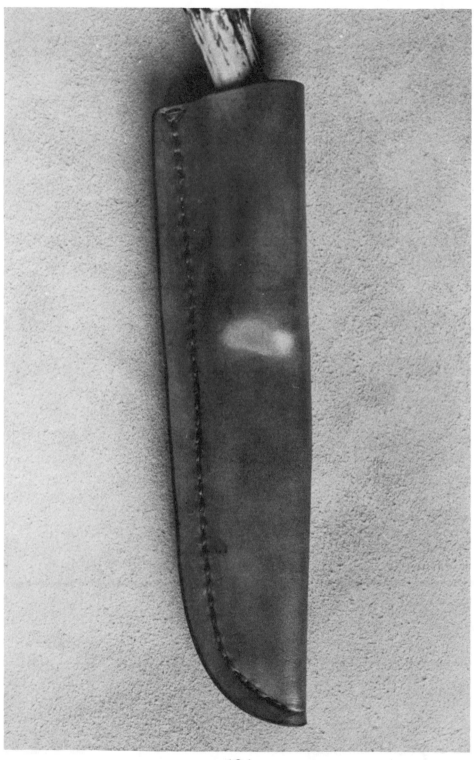

Knife Sharpening

Knife sharpening is at the same time the easiest thing to explain to someone, but the hardest thing for them to execute. I have spent much time explaining the technique to a wide variety of people and the experience has only reinforced the desire to present the following with the greatest wishes for good luck to those who will patiently stick with it and practice the art of sharpening a knife until they are masters.

The only way that I have found to effectively sharpen a knife is on a sharpening stone that is firmly mounted on a bench.

Basically, there are two types of sharpening stones commonly available. There are the natural stones, i.e., those of novaculite rock and those that are man made from abrasives heated in electric furnaces.

The natural stones are finer in nature than the man made stones. I prefer to use them as finishing stones. The most common types are the washita, and hard and soft Arkansas. Of the three the finest is the hard Arkansas. The other two are much softer and are the ones that I most often use.

The man made stone that I most commonly use is a combination of two abrasives. One side is aluminum oxide with a trade name of smooth India. The second is made of silicon carbide with a trade name of coarse crystolon.

With all of these stones I use mineral oil to suspend the particles of steel and abrasives when I am sharpening a knife. The oil keeps the pores of the stone from filling with particles that would eventually stop the cutting action of the stone. The oil should be wiped from the stone after its use. Occasionally, I scrub the stone with soap and water to further clean the pores. When dry, I restore the oil to the stone.

The object of sharpening is to lightly grind the edge of the knife over and over at the same angle to establish an even bevel or angle on both sides of the blade.

After pouring enough oil on the stone to cover its surface, place the knife blade flat on one end of the stone with the guard nearest the stone. Now place the thumb near the guard and extend the fingers of the left hand onto the blade up to the tip. I hold the knife with my right hand firmly and elevate the blade until the side of the edge is resting on the stone. Now push on the blade firmly with the fingers and at the same time draw the knife across the stone. If the angle is too high, it is almost impossible to move the blade. If the angle is too low, the blade will have scratch marks on it. With some practice, the right angle for the particular knife that you have will emerge. Note: Notice the position of the knife on the stone and the position of fingers on the blade.

The blade is then turned over and, with the fingers in position, the blade is pushed into and drawn back across the stone. This operation is repeated over and over at the same angle with the fingers at the same position. The most important things are the pressure when the blade is pushed into and across the stone and the holding of the same angle after each pass. Be sure that plenty of oil is on the stone at all times during the sharpening.

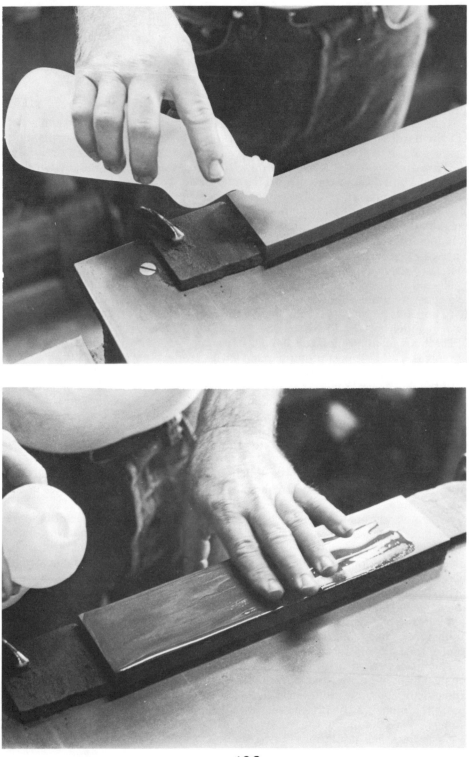

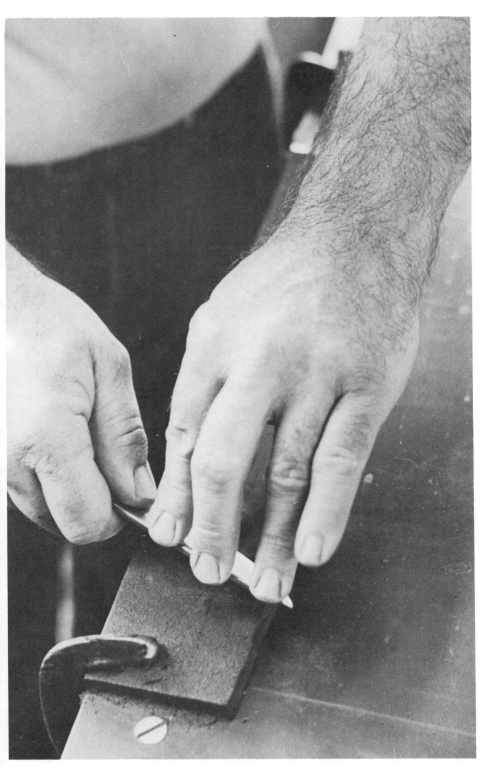

If the knife is dull, as most are in the kitchen, start your practice with the coarse crystolon, then to the India and on to the soft Arkansas stone. If you are pressing firmly and evenly on the blade you will begin to develop an even, sharp edge from the guard to the point. If this is not happening, then look for scratches (blade too low) or an uneven line that indicates uneven pressure of your fingers.

In general, the man made stones work better on the higher alloy steels, i.e., stainless. The abrasive material in these stones is harder and matches the carbide forming alloys. The natural sharpening stones put a smooth surface on the edge just like a fine sand paper. They are best used for the final sharpening or for the touching up of an almost sharp knife.

The advantage of hand sharpening with a stone is that a very small amount of steel will be removed from the knife edge. Grinding the edge of a knife should be reserved for those knives with thick, heavy blades that have been improperly made in the first place, and which cannot be adequately sharpened on the bench stone. Even then, it is extremely difficult to put a good edge on a knife with a grinder. I have seen knives sent out to be sharpened that returned permanently ruined from over grinding. Anyone with a reasonable amount of coordination can learn to sharpen a knife.

The size, width, and especially the length of the stone is important. Short stones are handy for carrying on trips etc., but are completely inadequate when trying to sharpen a long bladed knife. I strongly recommend getting the longest, widest stone that you can; 8x2x1" would be minimal and 11-1/2x 2-1/2x 1" better. These stones are available in most hardware stores or good cutlery stores. Long stones are not only more versatile, but much more stable than short ones. Ideally, the stone should be secured in a box or anchored so

that it will not slip. If these are not available, I have found that a damp towel placed on the cutting board will prevent the stone from slipping.

There is no need to have dull knives when it is so easy to sharpen them. A dull knife is a hazard in two ways; it causes accidents by having to force your way through the object and thus raises your frustration level, which causes more accidents.

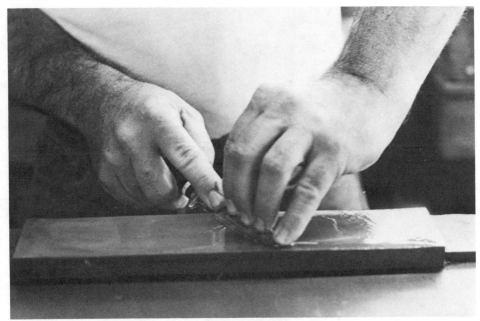

131

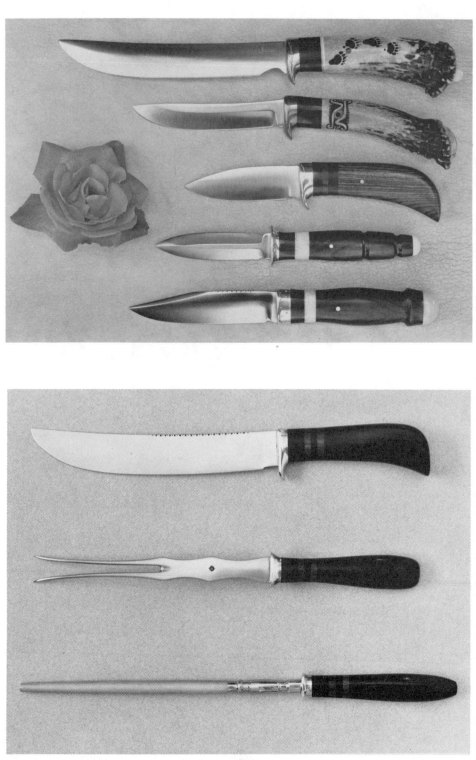

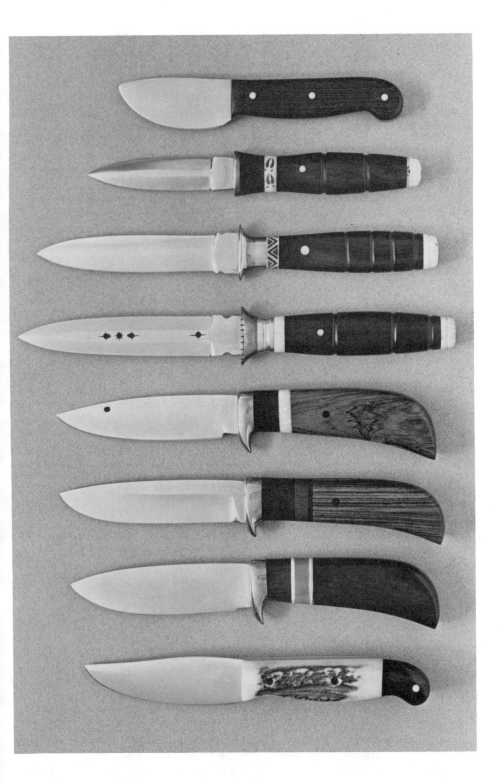

Annotated Bibliography

To my knowledge there are no books in or out of print that evaluate the full range of modern tool steels applied to ancient blacksmithing techniques. There are other books available on the general subject of knifemaking, but I did not use any of them in the composition of this series. What follows is a list of books that I did use and feel have value to any one interested in understanding the metalurgy of modern tool steels. The main source of current and past information in the field of metalurgy in general is the American Society for Metals in Metals Park, Ohio. The various tool steel companies have technical manuals which I will review in general terms since they are all so similar in content:

Alloying Elements in Steel, Edgar C. Bain and Harold W. Paxton (Metals Park, Ohio: American Society for Metals, 1966). This book gives technical information which stresses that alloys elements influence the properties of steel through their influence on rates of reaction. The book gives information gained from the electron microscope and other new tools of science. Prior knowledge of the subject matter is essential in order to get full advantage of this book.

Forging Equipment, Materials, and Practices, T. Altan, F.W. Boulger, J.R. Becker, N. Akgerman and H.J. Henning (Metals Park, Ohio: American Society for Metals, 1973). This book is a series of articles that deal with modern industrial forging. I used the book to verify, by scientific evidence, some observations that I made while experimenting with tool steels. The book is also valuable to those interested in contructing trip hammers and dies.

The Making, Shaping and Treating of Steel, Ed. by Harold E. McGannon (Pittsburgh, Pennsylvania: United States Steel, 1971). This book is a comprehensive overview of steel making and the steel industry. It discusses coal and where it comes from, iron and where it comes from and how it is converted to steel. Much of the book is devoted to a detailed description of steel plant construction and operation. Tool steel is discussed in detail. The only real criticism of this book that I have is the way in which it was written. The content is sometimes obscured and confused by overly complex sentences. The book is valuable in that it covers so much territory in a very thorough way.

Metals Handbook, ASM Handbook Committee (Metals Park, Ohio: American Society for Metals, 1961 8th Ed. This handbook comes in eleven volumes and covers every phase of metalworking. volumes 1, 2, and 5 are of particular interest to the traditional blacksmith, covering properties and selection, heat treating and forging. I have found that the 8th edition volumes, located in some county libraries, are written in clear, simple language that is easily understood. This handbook with its numerous volumes is continously being revised with the latest information. (Vol. 1, 9th Ed. 1978).

Tool Steels, G.A. Roberts, J.C. Hamaker, Jr. and A.R. Johnson (Metals Park, Ohio: American Society for Metals, 1962). This book is the most complete book on tool steels that I have yet seen. It has proved invaluable to me in the exploration of modern tool steels.

Properties of Imported Tropical Woods, Francis Kukachka (Madison, Wisconsin: USDA Forest Service Research Paper FPL 125, March 1970). This pamphlet will help those that are confronted with a wide array of tropical hardwoods found in speciality lumber yards, and wood working shops. Workability, strength, and durability are discussed for more than 100 tropical genera of hardwoods.

One item not mentioned in this pamphlet is cost. These woods are very expensive. In fact, more expensive than high quality tool steel. Some woods i.e., Wenge, Pau Brazil are not mentioned in this pamphlet.

Technical Manuals

Technical data manuals are put out by tool steel companies to explain the properties and the use of their product. Used in conjuction with other reference material, they aid the smith in the selection of the proper material. I have found them helpful; however, they are geared for industrial applications and need some interpreting. For example, the times and temperatures are for electric, or gas ovens, etc., and not coal forges. I have found that the forge heats up much faster than these ovens. Instead of hours, it may take minutes. The temperatures are not related to incandescent colors, and unless you have had lots of experience, you will need a high temperature sensing device such as a pyrometer to give accurate readings. (Note: Pyrometers are available in ceramic supply stores and scientific supply shops.)

The manuals lack any trouble shooting tips necessary if something goes wrong. These manuals may be obtained by contacting local outlets of the following tool steel producers:

Allegheny Ludlum Steel Corp., Div Allegheny Ludlum Industries, Inc., PO Box 152, Dunkirk, NY 14048.

Atlas Steels Co., A Div. of Rio Algom Mines Ltd., Welland, Ontario, Canada.

Bethlehem Steel Corp., Bethlehem Pennsylvania 18016.

Braeburn Alloy Steel Div., Continental Copper and Steel Industries, Inc., Braeburn, Lower Burrell, PA 15068.

Carpenter Technology Corp., PO Box 662, Reading, PA 19603.

Columbia Tool Steel Co., Lincoln Hwy, and State St., Chicago Heights, IL 60411.

Crucible Speciality Metals Div., Colt Industries, PO Box 977, Syracuse, NY 13201.

Latrobe Steel Co., Latrobe, PA 15650.

Teledyne Vasco, PO Box 151, Latrobe, PA 15650.

Universal Cyclops Specialty Steel Div., Cyclops Corp., 650 Washington Rd., Pittsburgh, PA 15228.

Jessop Steel Company, Washington, PA 15301.

Simond Steel Div., Wallace Murray Corp, Lockport, NY 14094.

The Timken Co., 1835 Dueber Ave., SW, Canton, OH 44706.

The following references are intended to open further avenues of discovery to those individuals interested in the subject of cryogenics.

1. Deep Cryogenics: The Great Cold Debate., Thomas P. Sweeney Jr., February 1986, Heat Treat Magazine. (Note: "Heat Treating" is a magazine of the metals heat treating industry published by The Fairchild Business Publication. Their address is 7 East 12th Street, New York, NY 10003.)

2. "Frozen Tools", Elaine Gilmore, Popular Science, June 1987.

3. Amcry International, 1613 West Burbank Blvd., Burbank, CA 91506. Amcry Cryogenics, 220 W. Chicago Ave., East Chicago, IN 46312 Technology, Inc. II.

There are many small companies that have started up to accomodate those industries that are convinced of the benefits of cryogenics.

Conclusion

The combination of modern tool steel with traditional blacksmithing techniques has just begun. I hope to stimulate an understanding of this material since I believe that only through a thorough knowledge of this material can a bladesmith take full advantage of it as a medium. I will continue to work with these materials and explore new ways of adopting them to the ancient techniques of blacksmithing.

I am indebted to two organizations: CBA, the California Blacksmith's Association; and ABANA, The Artist Blacksmiths' Association of North America for their support and encouragment.